ultimate
EQUIPMENT

forallthehighclimbingsure
footedslowstrollinglong
walkingtrendsettingeasy
movingcoolheaded
confidenceyouneed.

The Butts, Warkworth, Morpeth, Northumberland NE65 0SP
England. Telephone Warkworth (066 588) 413 or 453
Designers and Manufacturers
Lightweight tents, shell clothing,
the Ultimate climbers helmet and the Ultimate crampon

AA★★   RAC★★

Glenspean Lodge Hotel, Roy Bridge
INVERNESS-SHIRE
Telephone SPEAN BRIDGE 224

The hotel stands in its own grounds 2 miles east of Roy Bridge on the A84 overlooking Monessie Gorge. The hotel is warm and tastefully decorated with an excellent cuisine. Shooting and fishing are available by arrangement and there are unrivalled opportunities in the neighbourhood for hill walking and rock climbing. There are laundry and good drying facilities available to guests.

Resident Proprietors: Mr & Mrs NEAL MACPHERSON SMITH

ing nuts into the crack gave security for a tension which was effected as fast as shaking knees would allow, and led to a small hidden ledge beneath a thin crack. The ledge was belayless and the crack shallow, leading up to unknown ground but at least away from Hammer's awful drop. Possibly this was the 'crucial crack' mentioned in the guide, but anyhow it was climbable and led leftwards into a groove. Sickle's corner was still a long way off, but the climbing was of increasing quality, and even enjoyable despite the ice tongues. The first sign of humanity came in the form of an old rusty peg, well used by all appearances but still a good runner. From here a blank slab provided us with the crux, requiring pure friction before easing off into a scoop. A left traverse now led obviously to another groove which was descended and took us at last to the small trees in Sickle's corner.

This haven heralded the end of the climb and the ebbing of the sense of tension. The wall above, via cracked blocks and a short traverse, led to the edge of a huge crevassed flake, deep enough to camp in and a strange find on the Slabs. By going left we finished the climb on the easy sloping ground near the burn, now liberally iced and making the descent in P.A's about GRADE II.

Thus the Message grew from 210 to 355 feet, inclusive of the 55 feet of Sickle and gave a very varied and enjoyable route despite the ice and initial forebodings. Back at the sacs we found the place deserted and, with the twilight fast approaching, the Slabs looked magnificent. Gone was the 'outcrop' image of a warm summer's day and instead they seemed impossibly steep, sculpture on a vast scale, sombre and impregnable. However, the saga finally ended in the doctor's surgery where cold feet were diagnosed as minor frostbite. It took over a week before feeling was fully restored.

WET.

A change of partners and of scene took Alan Craig and myself to the Brack. This depressing north face has Arrochar's longest and most impressive lines, but suffers from a chronic lack of sunlight and a surfeit of vegetation. This sad state was not immediately visible from the road but became apparent the closer we approached. Our ambitions finally collapsed when the New Route terminated at thirty feet with a shuffle into Great Central Groove.

Despite two sweaters and an anorak, the wet was slowly penetrating but since the climb was only Mild V.S. 'when dry,' we assumed that it might 'go' in the wet. The first chimney was more like the fabled Hanging Gardens; long unpleasant green things spouted icy water when pressed and the Guide Book's preamble about Grand Struggles, Muck and Loose Rock became increasingly like a bad joke. The exit right from the chimney to the belay platform, probably about Very Difficult when dry, now bristled with slimy moustaches which even the redoubtable and hortophiliac Doctor* might have shunned.

The Groove now formed an ominous curving ramp, rising out of sight with water pouring liberally down. Ever optimistic, I brought Alan up, his exit from the chimney taken with all the aplomb of an oversized Water Baby. Though we (suckers), did not realise it, such antics were to become the norm higher up. Well belayed by Alan, the bulge was laybacked on good holds whilst the cracks of Mammoth overhung above, unfairly dry.

Over the bulge the waterlogged nature of the Groove became all too real and the 'easy climb' became committing since no protection was immediately available. An enormous stride right seemed the only way past a particularly nasty weepie and with Alan out of sight the world shrank to a long and rather nasty groove topped by a threatening block.

It is a sad fact that P.A's and wet schist are not good bed-fellows and the only way I avoided aerobatics was to use a handkerchief, tenderly drying the rock before placing each P.A. Such stomach-lurching procedures were partially allayed by a reasonable nut, but took me to, or rather through, the ultimate weepie. Things came to such a pass that I mounted my knees, prayed a little, then carried on laybacking on my knees since they provided more friction. Gingerly approached, the overhung block, despite its appearances, provided some good holds. Above, a small but awkward inset led to a recessed nook into whose welcome haven crawled a chastened, moss-covered figure.

This was undoubtedly the nadir of the climb and it was now cold as well as wet and further progress seemed doubtful. Rumbling protests reached me from below, and sagging miserably back into my wet chimney the thought flashed through that retreat was advisable. However, this temporary flash of sanity soon passed and in reply to Alan's enquiries I sent down a few croaks and a whistle (laryngitis had now set in). Alarmed no doubt that I had meta-morphosed into the Frog Prince, he arrived in a gallop of slithering P.A's.

United at last and the situation explained, I left the dank belay, stepping down and across to gaze into the maw of the foulest of green chimneys. Narrow and bulging in its lower parts it ran with water and we were almost persuaded to throw in the proverbial towel. However such defeatist ideas now seemed craven and I plunged onward. A strenuous grapple followed, leading to a ledge above which the corner rose vertically for 60 feet, reputedly the crux. When tackled I soon realised that the holds were so positive that the

---

*'The Craggie,' see S.M.C.J., 1975, xxx.

damp hardly altered the grade and it proved the easiest pitch of the route. Some delightful climbing led past Big Bill's threaded sling (relic of the winter ascent), and with this as a weak runner, I launched into the hole beneath the chock only to be brought short with a jerk. The rope had jammed below. The usual frustrating score or so attempts to free it were not needed, as with the first flick it came clear. I knew at last that St. Thadeus, the patron saint of Lost Causes, was at my side and the battle was virtually over. The climb finished by laybacking a little corner, which was dry, followed by a pleasant scramble through a narrow gully beneath an overhanging right wall.

We raced to the Brack's summit, having taken six hours, undoubtedly the slowest time ever. Drying off in the afternoon sun, we persuaded ourselves, the way climbers do, that we had really had a great time and might even do the route again—in the dry.

HOT.

The wet disappeared during the August heatwave and with Alan once more, I headed for the Cobbler one scorching Sunday. The walk up generated a sort of inverted glacier lassitude, with the initial slog up the Succoth ramp sheer purgatory. Even the stones appeared to sweat and mirages of water kept reappearing, causing spurts of increase in our stumbling rate, followed by relapses and incoherent mutterings as they faded.

With the dam gained and thirst assuaged, we began to appreciate the total lack of cloud, the endless blue, and the jagged rocks of the Cobbler spiking the skyline above. We pondered our day's menu: Deadman's Groove should surely be dry and out of the sun—a not unimportant fact—but the much finer Gladiator's Groove seemed too good to miss, since the rock was dry. Still undecided after the traditional tether by the Narnain boulder, we headed too soon towards South Peak and ploughed through still damp bog aiming for the haven of shadow underneath Bow and S Crack. Sick with heat, we reached this blissful shadow and rested to cool off, wondering what they did in Yosemite in even hotter conditions. The hill was nearly empty and gazing towards North Peak we saw a leader floundering on Punster's crux, smitten with heat and sweaty palms while trying to cross that wretched gap.

An enthusiastic jangle of gear and super glow-red helmet betokened the presence of Peter (ever youthful) Hodgkiss and friend returning from Ardgartan Arête and seeking shade like ourselves. Informed of a slight breeze on the west face our choice immediately swung to Gladiator's Groove as the day's main course. Gathering gear, we headed towards the sun and the west face ignoring easy options en route. Instant surprise appeared on the faces of an embracing couple as we rounded Ardgartan Arête and we amused ourselves at the thought of their arduous penetration of wilderness, in their search for a privacy so rudely shattered at the eleventh hour by the curious and vulgar.

The pool near the direct start had shrunk to a dirty black puddle and I half expected a rusty Excaliber to be raised; but had to settle for a prosaic Alan pointing meaningfully upward instead. I reckoned that if we climbed fast I could get Alan to snap the courting couple and sell them the negative, but the thought of sternly raised S.M.C. eyebrows drove the idea from my head and I concentrated on the climb instead. The direct start was a Bill Smith and Hope creation of 1952 and provides a superb approach of consistent standard and quality to the grooves above. A little bulge of quartz at twenty feet, gave the crux of this first pitch, leading runnerless to a fine stance and thread belay. So far the climbing was strenuous but the heat was modified by the odd snatch of breeze. United on the ledge, we caught sight of the couple again and once more they headed downwards, their resentments being audibly directed at our innocent selves.

Turning back to the rock, the second pitch was to provide the meat of the matter and the little black puddle suddenly seemed rather meagre. The idea is to traverse a thin ledge and when it vanishes, to step across a steep blank slab to the safety of a big block. Encouraged by a spike runner at foot level I headed rightwards. Physically, of course, it was simple. Use the quartz ripple for one hand and slide the right foot ever forward to a sloping hold and thus to better grip; but the puddle became even blacker and the incantations from the courting couple more ominous. A sudden commitment and I was across. It was easier than it looked, but was as exciting and delicate as the first pitch had been strenuous. Belays above were not of the best and when Alan followed, graphic descriptions of them caused the rope to vibrate. At the stance we saw the couple retreat for the last time and wished for a tele-photo lens, but the best opportunities are invariably marked by an empty camera.

Peter Pan had reappeared and under such a critical eye the pitch appeared to steepen. In the manner of a scrutineer he began to wield cameras, notebooks, stop watches, and the like, in order to intimidate me. Duly intimidated I crossed the rock and tackled the steep cracked corner. This looks awkward but is climbed relatively easily and leads to a small exposed ledge beneath the crux of the climb. A thin corner lies above, ending in a sloping shelf, and exuding that aura of difficulty normally associated with cruxes. The fixed, and perhaps original, piton was largely rust and had been supplemented by an angle, placed in such a way that it obscured the one good right hand hold. The activity below indicated that con-siderable interest was being shown. Provocative remarks about the steepness, difficulty and so on of the climb, did little to help my attempt to layback the right edge and establish a precarious jam in a hole above. As the jam was slowly unjamming a voice called out a carefully timed query about how to work the cine camera.

The platform above is holdless, sloping at 10° or so, but there is a little flat hold, if you know where to look, which enables a hurried mantleshelf ending (for me) on all fours. The belay, typically, wobbled but provided security to bring up Alan. He came on with suspicious speed, but was brought up short at the platform's lip by the prospect of a pendulum. More cautiously, he launched successfully onto the ledge. Above lay a steep crack, but the route itself took the overhung corner to its right utilising comforting holds to gain a superb and airy ledge beneath a bulging final crack. This was highly exposed but technically straightforward and gave a tremendous finish to end on the wide shelf above Ardgartan Arête.

Such is Gladiator's Groove. When coupled with the Direct start it is arguably the finest V.S. on the Cobbler and very worthwhile for any visiting climber. With the peg in the corner it is well protected and spurning its use as aid (naturally) we found that to be the crux rather than the mantleshelf, although both are hard, yet enjoyable.

At this juncture we realised the weather wheel had gone full circle. We had gone from freezing on the Slabs to frying on the Cobbler, with near drowning on the Brack in between, and that had been the rock climbing season. What on earth would winter inflict on us?

THE BEGINNING AND END

By Martin Henderson Moar

WE ARRIVED in red. I watched the heat smother everything. From the brown sand to the scorched rocks above. From the translucent surface of the water to the hot mud on the tracks beneath our feet as we left the bay. High above, the slopes burned, the river boiled down and turned between the parched heather.

We moved silently along the valley, stripped down so that the sweat ran down our backs and the heat bore down on our shoulders. We walked only as far as we wanted to. Then stopping, we lay down by the side of the dust on the track, letting our heavy packs fall; letting the heat settle on us. In the distance two bronzed shapes winged the sky, circling above soon after, clawing figures there, carrying with them the cooler air. We did not stir, but remained with dry lips and hot, very hot faces. There were no clouds. What was not red was blue: clear and infinitely deep. As clear as glacier water, as deep as those stretches of sea you sometimes pass over on the West Coast, the boat pulling through the water and you suddenly feeling you're above an unfathomable depth.

He rose up after some time, lifted his sack onto his naked shoulders and wiped away the moisture from his face. And then the sun was obscured and I saw myself dark as the cold settled on me now. Walking on we passed the bridge; the blur of tall pines bleached with the heat; the large black boulders in the stream, the water slipping through there. Here particularly the river was deep, very brown, and imperceptibly moving. We passed slowly. Then on up the shimmering valley; past the rust of the heather, the screaming white of the stream further up and the solitary tree. Then suddenly we were there. We were at the place: the air rising and falling in the heat; the warmth sliding over us; the water flashing brilliantly.

We knelt down, tired. Our packs were still on our backs. It had been a long way, especially with the constant dryness of the air and the ubiquitous glare of the sun. It was fine to rest now: the high grass moving before us and the glow around us.

That night in the tent I thought of the other times spent here. The time that the mists rose over the river and the visibility was so reduced that only a few feet ahead were discernible. Black shapes would rise out of the greyness only to be edged between or scrambled over after a few minutes walk. Summits became cairns; rivers roarings; and sheep became hoofed devils slipping off the side of the mountain. Every sound was heard: it was though they were amplified by the greyness, and like the shadows of the rocks, pressed into the confined space surrounding you. That night in the darkness of the tent I thought of those things again, and heard the scrapings in the grass, the wind between the stones in the river, and in the distance the waves of the sea like breathing.

In the morning we waded the river and made our way up to the first belt of slabs. High above the rock was bronze with the early sun. But lower, in the shade of the hill, the rock was cold and purple.

We planned the route visually and started. The rock was good and rough, easy enough. He led most of the way, and we only exchanged information by looks or glances. Higher up I took the lead. I moved slowly, the shadow of the hill following me up and the heat of the sun now burning into me, my face and arms sore with the heat of it. Below the final pitch we sat and watched the other side of the valley. A small plume of cloud hugged the summit of the opposite peak, and again we saw those eagles turning in the air. Below and to the right a few deer were splashing in a glistening pool, their heads rising and falling like the surrounding heat.

We took the final section slowly. Arms stretched, fingers tight; minds savouring the exposure deliberately, and intensely. Nothing could detract from the moment: no substitute, artifact, or thought. The movement of a hand became movement; the heat of the rock became warmth; and the blue of the sky became the sea. And when it was over we held it for a second, grasping it, refusing it a place in the past. Soon it was gone, and when we both sensed it leave us we turned to the summit. A quietness pervaded the rocks and in the distance the eagles turned once more and then headed out to sea. In the moment it took to touch the cairn they were gone.

It was my first rockclimb on the island, and his last climb.

delegate

above the plains
mountains flourish,
white, distracting eyes
at intersections.

they are cold, frequently
dangerous, always
exhausting and when you come down
are still there.

then why climb them?
say your constituents
say the headbellies say
the paunchbrains not knowing
what it is to represent them

what it is to be the guest
dirty unapologetic
of even a minor pinnacle
of even a single poem.

© G.F.D.

NO PLACE TO GO

By Philip Gribbon

SATIATED with snow, Auld Dawg was slumped on a chair, coffee in hand, abstracted from reality. His tinkling team of the Popsie and Daft were unshackling in the porch.

All, the prisoners of the night, were huddled round the fire, draped in the blankets, flat on the bunks, cramped in the alcove, rasping blunt points and linking krabs, studying guide books and leafing girlie mags, shuffling cards and boiling water. The hut, chock-a-block, dirty dishes on the table, leaking buckets on the floor. To endure and survive, to live and let live. With a couple of exceptions . . . .

Stock still, two figures stood and exuded an air of cold inhospitality tinged with officious indignation. They spoke for everyone's benefit. 'Just pack up all your stuff, an' get out.'

'Who, me?' Dumbfounded, Auld Dawg sat up, but looking at them with innocent surprise he asked cautiously, 'What for?'

'We're booked in, an' there's too many people in the hut.' Couldn't be more obvious. Tell us something new. But what a pair! A real Big Cheese with a sidekick, rabbiting on to justify their stance, to produce their figures, to confirm their dates. They held the floor with a gallery of captive spectators.

Oh, what a day it had been, absolutely superb, crystal clear, breathless, sun-steeped, with the Ben, rampant with routes, just snow plaster amidst blue shadows. It was a Mountain spectacular: the show in the desolate wilderness. The cognoscenti hordes had toiled up Allt a'Mhuilinn, they had dotted the glen in early straggling caravans. The search 'n rescue teams had arrived by chopper: they had to check out their overnight list of missing climbers. There was a slow sextet benighted below Tower Gap and a disorientated duo buried in a snow hole. Tracks soon wove across pristine slopes, sounds seeped out of muffled recesses. The ice dancers went a-whacking with prehensile cheating sticks, pointing up the chimneys, the scoops and the walls, solo on the Green, pairs on the Comb, queues on the Curtain. Overhead at the sunlit run of the plateau the helicopter thrashed noisily in the motionless air, fidgeted, and was gone. A deep stillness permeated the corries: it was so quiet that you could hear ice chips frizzling on the rocks. Auld Dawg, in a steep branching gully lush with ice bulges and with its frosted sides festooned with glass, had clung, chopped, grasped, stepped, clung again, chopped some more, gasped, bridged, leaned, traversed, and sweated. Modern alloy crampons with front points were beyond his ken: ye canna teach Auld Dawg new tricks! He struggled up with sparse help from his antique castiron claws, until thankfully he reached an old peg. He always made a GRADE IV meal out of someone else's III. Quickly the Popsie stabbed on with her sharp points. They found sweet calm below the cornice until he led through its floundering fluff to a whipped-ice sastrugi bowl where the chilly spicules cascaded in a golden rustle out of the setting sun. Flimsy mists wafting rose up the slope, while beyond a double sun dipped into the haze on the sea beyond Morven and a full orange moon distorted like a ginger jar edged slowly above the distant Cairngorms. Thin translucent icicles shone like swords of fire on the cairn, while the cushions of snow, burnished like molten gold, were glowing cold. Only the silhouette of the Popsie was live warmth. She left following Daft, galloping in the furrow that he had ploughed through the crust towards the hut. Auld Dawg was the last in the stampede . . . .

Now he was listening with interest to a leading question spoken in a tone of partial disbelief. 'How do we know you're booked in?'

Well, that was a fine rhetorical question. It didn't warrant a straight answer and he didn't give it. The spectators were providing silent support for their choice of either the Home or Away team.

'If you're so sure of your ground, what's the password?' Normally the powers that be select the name of a route at random. In a do-or-die effort Big Cheese had deployed his trump card. If Auld Dawg said the magic word, then everyone was safe for the night.

'Password! What d'ya mean?' His defence was his attack. Perhaps he had forgotten it. Big Cheese quoted the book of rules while his sidekick waved a letter of introduction in the sultry air.

The letter was carefully folded to hide the password. 'Very interesting,' Auld Dawg commented, after a brief perusal. He saw that they were aware that he knew more than they had thought that he could have known about the running of the hut. They were losing, slowly but surely, but they wouldn't give up and kept doggedly on, inquisitive to the end. 'Well, are you in the J.M.C.S.?'

Auld Dawg gave his grizzled whiskers a contemplative scratch. They had made a legitimate mistake: some J.M.C.S. members had left the hut that afternoon. However, in spite of such flattery, he had to shake his head in rejection of their suggestion.

The inevitable, practically predestined, question waited in the air. It came out hesitantly, lurching from unhappy lips. 'You aren't, are you, a member of . . . . the S.M.C.?'

Yes, Auld Dawg nodded in slow affirmation. Inside he sensed a complex bundle of emotions that ranged from proud embarrassment to righteous abhorrence, but, most important of all, he had a knowledge of his ultimate victory. His tormentors had become the victims of their self-inflicted defeat. Their cause was lost. Big Cheese and his pal faded away to a dark corner. Three jolly cheers, everyone was in. Long live comfort and squalor.

'Well done,'—a just comment in a sincere whisper from a temporary resident. He had been saved from his early bed in a frigid tent.

Next day, the Ben alone floated above the cloud sea. Perfect, in sun sparkle, Auld Dawg met Big Cheese at the head of the descent gully.

'Sorry about the trouble last night,' Big Cheese murmured apologetically.

'Aw, that's O.K.', replied Auld Dawg diffidently. 'You did the right thing, y'know.'

Together they studied the boundless expanse of their sunny world stretching out to the horizon.

'Had a good day?' It was a man-to-man remark spoken with mutual respect.

'Aye, just great!' Auld Dawg smiled extravagantly, and with the Popsie in pursuit he leaped headlong down the snow.

THE BIG EYE OF SUMMER

By I. H. M. Smart

In the High Arctic there are long periods in summer when the weather is calm and cloudless. At such times the silence, clear light and brilliant reflections make previous experience unreliable. The detail visible on distant hills is such that twenty miles seem nearer two. The fjord waters mirror the stone hills and icebergs so exactly that seaplanes coming in to land cannot distinguish the essential interface between reflection and reality. A cry in the lowlands vanishes into the air like a stone disappearing into water without a splash or ripple, while a shout among the hills comes back from the planes of rock in multiple echoes of varying intonation whose loudness is often unrelated to the sequence of return.

The familiar sun, however, remains above the horizon all day, tracing an easily verifiable circle in the sky. This most reassuring fact is said to be an illusion. Astronomers and their equations seem happier if the moving sun is taken to be stationery and the solid earth rotating. Be that as it may, once during a period of settled weather our boat crossed the inner reaches of Scoresby Sound, threading its way along the narrow sea lanes between the hundreds and thousands of icebergs which are a feature of this area—mansions, palaces, and cathedrals of crystalline splendour daring and original in design and each meticulously repeated by its reflection in the still water, a silent white city fifteen miles across, the Summer Capital of the Winter King, built like others from the resources of its hinterland.

I was left on the shore near Gurreholm at the mouth of the Schuchert River while the boat returned vanishing Lethe-wards among the reflections. For reasons which need not distract us here I had to be 120 miles away as quickly as possible. This was no hardship; a man who finds himself to be healthy, alone, and free to travel lightly laden in the still emptiness of the High Arctic has been granted a high privilege.

The first leg of the journey lay across the level floor of the Schuchert River while the boat returned, vanishing Lethe-wards a point clearly visible five miles away through cotton grass haloed against the low sun induces a liberating tranquility. The mechanism of progress can be left to the spinal cord which enjoys an autonomy it has not had since the introduction of cephalisation. There are no navigational problems and the mind is free to join the landscape. After a succession of these five mile stretches the route left the valley floor and climbed up to the broad saddle leading to Ørsted's Dal and the sea. Here I stopped for a few hours' rest while the sun hung low over the northern horizon. The shadow of night lay far to the south with its edge over Scotland. In Greenland, however, it was the time of the union of opposites when there is no today and time hangs between the brocaded richness of yesterday's evening and the brave simplicity of tomorrow's dawn.

I was sitting opposite the broad Roslin Glacier. A dozen years before, the youthful Slesser and I made the first crossing of the unknown southern Staunings Alps and emerged down this mighty glacier after days of crevassed uncertainty and windy camps in the much serrated interior of the range. I remembered reaching the mouth of the glacier on an evening as serene as the present. We had, with growing confidence, become separated. Slesser had wandered off by himself and a mile of flat glacier lay between us, but such were the acoustics we could still argue distinctly by slow shouts. I remember the final shout 'C-a-l-l y-o-u-r-s-e-l-f a b-l-o-o-d-y e-x-p-l-o-r-e-r.' It echoed and re-echoed from the ranks of broken buttresses of bracken-brown granite, returning again and again in the glory of the golden evening, sometimes clear, sometimes fragmented; a scene where only man was vile and he was a mile off the route, too.

A decade later another expedition fought its way up the same glacier through the deep snow of early summer. After three days of heavy-laden struggle they reached their base camp in the promised land of an unknown side glacier deep in some inner sanctum of the range. Four prospectors were already there sitting round a table playing cards in front of a large, well-appointed tent with a helicopter parked suburbanly by its side. They offered these travellers from an antique ideology cups of coffee and kind smiles, fresh rolls and the latest news.

The route now wandered through a pleasant landscape of green meadows and blue lochans. Herds of musk oxen safely grazed among the poppies and sun-caught cotton grass. Skeins of well-rehearsed geese peter-scotted across the dawn sky. Legs, given their head, moved effortlessly, rhythmically, feet rattling against the yellow and white Draba flowers. The soul was free to take down interesting thoughts from the richly-stocked shelves of the mind, throw them up in the air and watch them sparkle in the clear morning light. This exhilaration stemmed from confidence in one's physical and mental ability to travel in empty lands, the perfectly tuned mind in the perfectly tuned body in an aesthetically perfect environment.

This lasted until noon. Time for a short nap. It was then I noticed an impulse to crawl head first into my sleeping bag, easily resisted but an odd desire, nevertheless. After a few hours rest I descended into the middle reaches of Ørsted's Dal. But something had changed. The landscape seemed to be taking note. The hills hemming in the valley were no longer mounds of indifferent stone to be patronisingly measured by the mind as being shapely or ugly, but seemed to have usurped the initiative and were taking cross bearings on my slow progress down the long valley. This feeling of being watched grew all afternoon. Every pebble stood out sparkling and crystalline in the clear light, each a cell in the great compound eye of the landscape. If only a tent were available to crawl into to reduce the visibility, or a cave to provide some privacy and escape from the singing breezes. You can't lie down to sleep in a whispering shop window or a room walled with one-way mirrors.

Towards evening the native hills drew back to leave a plain ten miles across. The golden light filled the early autumnal landscape up to the blue shadows of the northern hills. It would soon be time for supper and a relaxing dram before enjoying the ambience of the surrounding grandeur as one dropped off to sleep, tired by an unforgettable day's walk. The mind tried to board up the windows with the old familiar clichés but they kept falling off. Maybe it would be better to cross the Pingo Dal river first, a few miles further on and nearer the hills. It would be easier to relax with this obstacle behind. It was reached effortlessly, passing on the way the gaze of a bright-eyed lochan surrounded by blue eye-bright (*Euphrasia frigida*) and the Argus-eyed inflorescences of the arctic primrose (*Primula stricta*), the latter a rare plant in these parts. The river was bigger than I had expected. Its braided tresses sang in the sunlight and the far bank lay in cold shadow. Still, it would go with care and a safe route could be picked out among the gravel banks. The crossing was easy until an irreversible commitment had been made to the last stretch which turned out to be deeper and faster than it seemed. The sunlight shimmered on the dazzling, dancing, trilling water, so much more attractive than the cold gloom of the approaching bank. It would be so reasonable, so interesting, to yield to the eager insistent pressure of the thrilling, lifting water and discover the origin of all the excitement. Legs, however, kept moving ahead, gripping the river bed, unmoved by the heady fire water. Then into the shadow; the jewels turned to lead and the seductive laughter to splashing water.

After the trembling and the cold sweat had passed and the hair on the nape of the neck lay flat, I sat in the shadow of the valley, back against a boulder in the protection of a sleeping bag looking southwards to where the warm brown moorland of Ørsted Dal lay combing its golden hair in the sunshine. To the left crouched the lowering pack ice with its wandering bears and unpredictable ways. Behind and to the right the dark and drublie hills still lacked their usual indifference as if they sensed that the action had gone wrong. Nearer hand clumps of *Saxifraga stellaris* starred the dark tundra— a tenuous link with the past, for they also grew light years away at home. Time to take stock—the clichés were beginning to run out.

The Big Eye is a well known phenomenon in the Arctic, characterised by sleeplessness and the feeling of being constantly watched. The mind usually does a good job to protect its owner from the pressure of surrounding things; the unknown is efficiently silvered over to give comfortable reflections of the familiar. In lonely open places without the constricting resonance of a companion or any sign of human artefact the expected reflections return only weakly. The silvering begins to dissolve, and bright undefined things come through and create a debatable land of possessor and possessed. The searing nakedness of that which is there becomes too much for eye and mind. Exploration of this territory is an unchancy business, and in moments of emergency survival depends on the immeasurably greater experience of sub-cerebral reflexes. It is no time to have a beginner in the driver's seat.

After six hours' rest, the journey continued through a range of Torridon-type mountains into the next broad valley turning red and gold under the first frosts of autumn. Then another night passed in a gloomy pass, but controlled this time with the frontier better defined. Another day in the silent land and I was safely back at the Danish weather station at Mesters Vig, back in the kindergarten again with the old familiar pictures on the wall. The walk seemed to have taken a long time, but measured by the schoolroom clock it had lasted half an hour under three days.

AVALANCHED!

By Sandy Cousins

'Cousins in Full Flight'

THRILLING, frightening, comic, tragic—an avalanche is all of these. Due to our misjudgment of snow condition I was caught in one and maybe the experience will be of use to others.

My tale begins at Corrour Bothy in the Cairngorms. Our party was on a two-day ski tour enjoying good Easter conditions of ample snow cover following the heavy fall of the previous few days. We skied from Achlean to Corrour in sunshine and occasional mist. Next morning the blasts of wind which rattled the bothy during the night had died down and we emerged into cold calm sunshine. The Lairig Ghru was carpeted wall-to-wall by firm snow, a joy to ski. We skinned easily up the pass on smooth snow many feet deep over the Pools of Dee and by noon we were passing the March Burn which was completely snowed over. From the top of the Lairig we looked through to the Sinclair shelter and Rothiemurchus forest, bathed in sunshine.

Various alternative routes to gain the west corner of the Cairngorm plateau were discussed and finally we chose to climb out of the Lairig about half a mile west of the March Burn to gain the top of the Allt Creag an Leth-choin and thereby have a fine three-mile run down to the Glenmore forest. There had been no snow for two or three days but the slope above held a lot, the horizontal sastrugi showed there had been some wind-packing, though generally it was soft so that one sank over the ankle without ski. We chose to climb the strips of frozen scree for better footing. Our party was what the Press would call 'very experienced and well equipped,' but there was no mention, or I believe, even thought, of avalanche. Later of course it was obvious the new snow had fallen on old hard snow in freezing conditions with no subsequent thawing and freezing to key the whole thing together. Here was an obvious case for pondering the conditions prevailing for the few days *before* one's climb and our mistake was in not realising we were 'standing into

Photos: G. S. Strange

Route I   Winter on the Black Spout Pinnacle of Lochnagar—January 1977   Route II

Eagle Ridge, Lochnagar—first pitch   June 1976

Photo: W. D. Brooker

danger.'

And so we climbed with our ski on our packs. Well up the frozen scree slope half our party took to the snow, plodding deep steps up a shallow gully about twenty feet to the right of the little ridge the rest of us climbed. I led up a short steep section and found the ridge levelling off as the head of the gully swept up in a steep snow-wall. Above the slope rolled back in a series of snow waves. Some of my group seemed to find the steep section a little difficult so I moved right to walk up the deep snow close to the right of the ridge. The first man of the other group was just climbing out the side of the gully up the snowy grass opposite me. His followers were plodding up the gully and my group were close behind me, the last man still on the ridge.

Suddenly I sank back, took a couple of steps up and with a sickening feeling realised that I was on a moving mass of snow— Avalanched!

I learned later that the last man in the gully group had seen a crack open in front of him and away he went thinking he was the only one, so the whole mass had started simultaneously. I remember thinking as I sank into the snow, 'Oh, Christ, you mug, avalanched!' With no time to look round I glimpsed the sunlit crest close on my left leaping away upward as I sagged into a moving snowy mattress. I rammed my ski sticks through the snow seeking a hold but everything was on the move, accelerating fast. My ski were down the loops at the side of my pack, clipped together at the tips above my head. Some had theirs across their packs or up the side and they suffered most damage. Almost immediately I was rotating and tumbling past our steep section. I felt myself falling a short way, then I was on my front, head down, flying in a confusion of snow. Some rasped my throat and I remembered, 'don't inhale snow' so I held my mitt across my face, sucking air through my teeth. Now I was bowling down on my front, sometimes bouncing, in the dark grey world inside the avalanche. I wondered if the others were alright somewhere around me or if I was on my own. Remembering the slope below was an open snow slope, free of pitches and rocks, I thought is might be best to get as far down as possible in case the tons of snow behind should bury me. Some time ago in a winter climbing fall I had done some seven hundred feet down a gully and I hoped my God and my luck were with me again. That time my companions had lost their axes and mine had broken but I was able to stop us all using an ice-spike I had, but this time I knew I was at the mercy of the snow. I paddled with my elbows to keep the snow loose around me and kept my legs together to prevent damage from flailing about. My head was between my ski thus protected a bit, and I held my sticks across before me to ward off any bumps. I found myself saying, 'relax man, save energy in case a real burst is needed to dig upward.' Since my initial burial I had been almost holding my breath and just as I wondered how long until I had a chance for clear air I burst into white light momentarily and gulped air through my mitts, then I was covered again. Snow was tumbling around me and once I felt it begin to pack so I immediately kicked and elbowed to keep it loose. However, I was still moving, and then, as suddenly as I had slid backwards probably less than a minute ago, I tumbled out into bright sunshine and stillness.

Looking up in case debris was still following I saw a large area of jumbled blocks and the empty swept slope above. I stood up, dropped my pack, noting my ski seemed O.K. (I later found one tip slightly crimped), my limbs seemed alright and glancing at the blue sky I thanked God. Above me figures lay or stood around on the mound of debris. The snow blocks were rock-hard and several rocks had been torn from the gully. Two figures were still high on the hill, the man on the right had been left above the gully as the snow vanished behind him and the other on the left had been finishing our steep bit when he suddenly saw a tangle of arms, legs and ski flash past him in a cloud of snow. I yelled at them to count us and heard seven were visible, so no one was buried. The fracture of the slab avalanche ran right across the head of the gully including some of the slope above the crest we had been climbing. Judging by the figures there the wall was at least fifteen feet high in the gully and some hundred feet across. It had swept the slope clean. One of the party had fallen through the avalanche and had been dumped on the scree after only a few feet. The debris had come to rest about fifty feet above the floor of the Lairig and I estimate our speed was some twenty miles an hour down six hundred feet (vertical) at maybe forty-five degrees, amongst about five hundred and thirty tons of snow.

Knox and Sandy made their way down to us joining Andy in the gully. Hugh lay a hundred feet above me not moving and near him Graham sat holding his head as a large red stain spread down his pullover. I tried to walk up to Graham but my legs would hardly move and I found my elbow becoming warm and sticky from a cut. We all felt we had been through a mangle. Hugh stirred and staggered down with Graham and I bandaged the long cut in his head. Tom came down, blood dripping from his sleeve and Hugh diagnosed a smashed elbow which he bound. Ken was worst hit, head, back and arm being hurt, so Bill, Andy and Knox put him in a sleeping bag in a tent. Three chaps who had seen our slide from the Lairig came across and gave very competent help. Several ski were smashed and packs ripped. We considered a ski-sledge for Ken but our two doctors were reluctant to risk rough handling. Regretfully, I suggested I ski down to call for assistance from the staff at Glenmore Lodge. At this stage we hoped to get a sledge and take our friends down ourselves.

Ski touring is part of mountaineering and as such one must

AVALANCHED!

accept its risks, however serious. Rescue is not something one should automatically expect and I feel that self rescue should always be considered first, even though the decision is finally taken to call for outside help in the interests of the casualty.

I reckoned on one and a half hours to reach the Rothiemurchus hut then with say three hours to return we could make it in daylight. Hugh and I set off on ski. One group stayed with Ken and one group walked Graham to the Sinclair bothy—hard going in deep snow. At the hut Fred Harper's reassuring voice on the phone was welcome. He soon had the information and a chopper was on its way, diverted from another avalanche call which had come earlier from Coire an Lochain. Hugh arrived very tired and the folk at the hut were very helpful.

In the busy moments spent at Glenmore Lodge as the helicopter was briefly there I am sure our sincere thanks were hardly noticed so from us all I give them again to both the helicopter people and the Lodge staff involved.

Soon Ken and Tom were on their way to hospital, young Graham was stitched and we walking cases dispersed to hobble around like old men.

SNAW BA'S

By Roger O'Donovan

A few established facts. If one excludes the nonsense of individuals who suffer from 'avalanching foot steps,' avalanches account for four per cent of all reported accidents on Scottish hills (Humble 1976). In January 1800, at Gaick a sizeable and celebrated mass buried a hut containing one Captain MacPherson of Kingussie, and his companions, while they were on a deer stalking trip. The event exercised tongues and pens (Hogg, The Etterick Shepherd, 1810, Sir Walter Scott, 1827, and Andrew Lang, 1891), created a Speyside myth, and caused to be erected an excellent little monument at the accident site. In 1893 the ubiquitous Raeburn encountered avalanches on two days running during attempts on the Centre Post of Creag Meagaidh. In 1902, Maylard accurately described slab conditions on Ben More, Perthshire—one of his party confirming the observation by a splendid minor involvement. On Beinn Achaladair in 1909 a roped party was engulfed—a reported Scottish first, and in December 1964 Robert Burnett was found alive on Beinn a'Bhuird after 22 hours burial. Two of his companions died. Records of deer killed by avalanches go back over two centuries.

To write confidently on the subject of avalanche occurrence in Scotland is like the blindfold juggling of a dozen eggs. The conflicting opinions of *experts* is as blushing, strident, and fragile on the topic as those on the weather or even on the nature of God himself. Practical graduates of the near-miss school may well be modifying their approach after years of gleeful play, but a new influence is displaying itself, I think for the first time. Potting shed pundits are avoiding the hills and advising others to do the same and the press and others bend an ear to their myopic and often pathetic utterances.

To attempt properly to advise, give warnings or useful rules of thumb for practical hill use is notoriously difficult. Most research currently being published concerns the conditions of dry Alpine snow. This is largely the work of theorists working with sand and slide rules, with frequent refutations by practical observers producing an ever obscurantist flow of often conflicting research papers from Russian, American and Swiss establishments; countries where avalanches have real economic significance. *Our* snow, good, temperate climate, mountain island, unfaithful snow, has not been adequately studied. Work by Eric Langmuir in the Northern Cairngorms was the first serious study—this in the late '60's. Sporadic work by others has trotted off into the all consuming territory of Thesis, or concerned itself with matters other than avalanche. No co-ordinated, all-embracing, national study has been initiated—Mr Avalanche has yet to be mobbed at a TV chat show.

Against such a background, broadcasts and notices have appeared in recent years . . . . 'Avalanche Warnings.' On average wild and exhilarating winter days such blanket statements as 'Climbers are warned to keep off the mountains' are appearing in the debris at the foot of certain newspaper columns (ironically this is published usually when winds have stripped the offending snow from ridges and most slopes and the sun now shines). Never has the writer heard of such a warning being cancelled. Despite some five or six days a week on the hill over the last four winter seasons and reasonable contacts throughout Scotland for twice that period, I have never heard of a snow scientist or observer been seen conducting anything like the kind of methodical observations and documentation which are absolutely fundamental to such confident diagnosis of a situation which is always complex and prone to rapid change.

When recently approached on the subject of avalanche warnings Marcel de Quervain (Director, Weissfluhjoch, Davos, Switzerland) and Ed la Chapelle (Washington University), reacted very cautiously. Without daily or even hourly observations and a local and specific data basis over *at least* five years, they could see no validity for any statements at all by anyone . . . . except possibly one expressed along the lines of a risk factor, like Littlewoods or Joe Coral. These two sensible avalanche researchers are men whose prudence and wrinkles enhance the obvious.

Should there then be finance and scholars urged on to the hills with a remit to report on *their* custody of the snows? Should our beloved National, Regional, Local or Tribal Big Brothers take it upon themselves to make the mountains safe for us all yet again? Doubtless, someone, some day, will argue for it. May it be suggested that this, like all such official lay lunacies regarding mountain accidents, hazards, the people and their fun is damn nonsense and futile for the Scottish situation. Avalanches occur as a natural part of the process of water going home to the sea. In all likelihood the frequency of avalanche occurrence has not increased in recent years (a favourite lay blunder), but the number of people on the hill has. In its various phases snow is sometimes stable but never static. Gravity and a continuous process of sloughing, sliding, leaching, ablating, subliming, re-subliming, shearing and creeping, melting, freezing and drying may effect any snow crystal on the ground on our hills. Many of these things occur more rapidly on south west slopes—prevailing wind; on south and east slopes—sun. An acceptable statement from this is that these slopes stabilise more rapidly—usually. Most climbing is done on north facing slopes however, where things develop more slowly. Consequently the destructive metamorphism or stabilisation process of snow takes longer. But two gullies within a hundred metres of each other can have reached very different stages on any given day—one may be completely safe with respect to avalanche release, the other ready for an unwary ptarmigan looking for a quick doss in an old footprint.

'Avalanches occur on slopes above 35 degrees.' A classical myth surrounds the supposed angles at which snow avalanches. Laboratory work has given slides of some significance at 7°. In the field it is often stated that between 20° and 60° one can expect avalanches (observably true) and since cornices hang at all angles the upper categories are catered for. So the people of the Fens are notoriously carefree about big white woofers—those who live in flat roofed houses that is.

To my knowledge, excluding those involving people, avalanche frequency has never been recorded accurately in any one area or even one choire. In spite of some very real sceptism it is hoped that some kind of regular observations will be carried out in the winter of 1976-77 by the Glenmore Lodge staff and local climbers, on at least two or three slopes of different aspect. This, together with some weekly snow bank studies, in selected locations, and the newly available continuous weather recording instruments on Cairngorm summit, could give a clearer local picture, or at least some indication for future work. Even assuming a successful programme one doubts its importance since it is strongly felt that intensely local phenonema are of predominant importance, and each year is notoriously varied with regard to wind patterns and precipitation factors. Information acquired will not in any way be geared to an advisory service.

What can the active mountaineer or off piste skier do to guard against becoming a snow accident statistic? To familiarise himself with the available literature on the subject and then relate this to his direct observations and experience seems logical. The occasional hunch about a slope may well be confirmed by a simple pit dug in the snow at the foot of the gully or slope in question—not too enthusiastic a pit since more than one seeker after truth has found the ultimate answer! The profile of snow layers revealed can display great variation of snow types and adhesion factors one to another— broadly speaking, what is found at the foot of the slope will pertain throughout its length. The relative 'hardness' of adjoining layers is the most importance factor to establish. This does not provide for the gully top where local wind effects may produce deposition conditions, knowledge of which must entail direct involvement or a look-see from above (a habit which could well exhaust the prospective climber's enthusiasm for the route, or even lead to some spectacular, if unhealthy, descents).

It might be worth commenting that in Scotland, broad scale avalanche conditions are comparatively rare, sometimes very beautiful and usually rather obvious. Localised full depth avalanches—like a snow slide from a pitched roof where the whole snow cover goes—occur on rock slabs, uniform grass covered slopes (village of Lewes, Sussex Downs, early 19th century), and some scree slopes. Again, these are not all that common and are usually in fairly obvious and locally known locations. The Great Slab, Coire an Lochain, is a classic of the genre. It is the sneaky wind slab at the head of a lee slope col, the cornice and the slab filled stream bed, that causes most alarm. Its bed sister, the partial depth slide, caused by alien layers accumulating or developing within the snow bank where the upper layer or layers slough off that poses the other subtle threat. A pit diagnosis is recommended.

One of the most underestimated factors from past records is the number of comparatively small localised slides which have literally knocked people from their footing and launched them on to a boulder field beneath. A friend, once avalanched, obeying the dictum of 'swim with the flow' actually outswam the snow debris of a slide and flailed off through a sizeable stretch of boulder-strewn slope—with appropriate results. (An apocrypha to this incident, is that the poor fellow actually triggered the thing off by having a pee whilst out of sight of some ladies of the party).

Why one takes an interest in these things might well stem from an unwary incident in the past, a thought-provoking near-thing to a companion, maybe even a morbid fascination; a kind of private game with a big white chicken. The active climbers I know vary from the totally blase to the morbidly cautious. Mostly, I believe, they accept that no snow can be completely trusted—think of any snow belay for a hairy runnerless ice pitch above. This understanding, the intuition, feel, sensibility, evaluation and judgment involved, are for me the essence of the winter climb.

The over-simple pronouncement is that which is most suspect. On an early spring day in 1975 I recall visiting the area of cliffs at the head of Loch Avon. Twenty-three different, comparatively recent, avalanche tracks were noted on slopes facing from due north round through east to due south. Six identifiable different types of avalanche were on show. From one, a metre wide surface slush slide which had fallen 300 metres to another two metres deep, 200 metres wide hard slab, which had run for 200 or 300 metres within a thousand metres of each other. There was also a cornice droop and crack, falling only two metres and a spectacular powder fan which started high in the Diagonal Gully of Stag Rocks and debouched out on to the frozen loch for a couple of rope lengths. And that was a clear day.

The late Dr Bell's statement that it takes about three winter seasons' experience before the climber can have an understanding of Scottish snow conditions seems eminently wise.

Note: For those who wish to accelerate or amplify their understanding there is no good source of reference dealing specifically with Scottish conditions; 'The ABC of Avalanche Safety' by Ed. La Chapelle is a really good general booklet and contains many references. It can be otained from Glenmore Lodge, current price £1·40.

Over 150 avalanches have been recorded in the Cairngorms during the past winter.

FLIES

By G. J. F. Dutton

'DAMN these blasted fles!' roared the Doctor, the hundredth time that day. The Apprentice, beginning a similar though more virile malediction, inhaled too great a horde of *Muscidae* and fell back speechless. For each of us, like an island peak, carried his own cloud. Dodging or ducking could never escape it. Bracken and branches beat in vain. Hands were blistered, arms ached. Chitinous and insistent, it clung. And it buzzed and crawled abominably. At times one of us would creep up to unload his cloud on to a companion; and then try to run free. But the companion, unencumbered—in fact, spurred—by the additional burden, would race to repay him. Heads were thrust under water: but on emergence proved even more attractive.

Walking up and walking down that year were enlivened by such performances, and we grew desperate. Camping was intolerable until darkness brought its relief and its midges—at least a familiar, almost hereditary, malady, benign by comparison. And even then the odd nocturnal fly padded damply across our faces. Driven by the horrors of reverberating sleeping bags and ham-and-fly suppers, we carried a tent—translucent with fly-squash and rustling with old wings—to the top of Ladhar Bheinn; but we left one pole in the Doctor's car, and it rained. Another weekend I gasped in a fly at an unpleasant move above The Chasm, and spat us both into space. Later that day the Doctor also came to grief, claiming he had slipped on a handful of the brutes—'like ballbearings on a slab.' At the top, the Apprentice solemnly declared he'd been forced to roll a cloud of them up into a convenient chockstone; it had brought the two of us over the crux before dispersing and flying away. They had in fact become part of the climbing scene. But we never got used to them. We would plot, plot in our downhill cursing. How *could* they be defeated?

Sundew, environmentally preferable, was too slow. We had tried flypaper. We hung three flypapers in the sleeve entrance of the Doctor's Mummery tent, and gloated on the speedy arrest of incomers. But we celebrated unwisely, because that night the Apprentice, wriggling out at the call of nature, forgot about the flypapers. His retreat into the alarmed and pitchblack tent, trailing flypapers and sleeve entrance, needs no elaboration. Fly-sprays were expensive, amused the flies and, according to the Doctor, ours (though not his) were dangerous to health. Nylon net bags did not fulfil their promise. They let feet through and leaked at the neck; and in driving one devil out we allowed seven more in. Ointments and suchlike merely provided the creatures with refreshment and an opportunity to linger.

We sat in despair that evening. Each spoke to the other out of his cloud. One learnt to communicate in this Jove-like fashion, through compressed and fly-denying lips.

'I got most of mine from that dead hind on the bealach' hissed the Doctor. This provoked unkind comparisons. The Apprentice observed, sideways, that next time he'd bring up some bad meat and lose all his flies on to that.

The Doctor sprang up. His cloud re-adjusted itself nimbly.

'Of course! Of course! What about that new chemical they've made? Better than anything so far known for attracting flies—they used it as bait to clear 'em out of Egyptian hospitals. Has a fearful pong. An improvement on some amine or other from a decomposing

mushroom. I know a chemist at the University. I'll get him to try
for some. Bound to work!' And he fell back contented into his
flies.

That Thursday in Daddy McKay's his eyes were alight.
'Astonishing luck. Chemist chap knew all about it. Had some
in the next lab. Musc-a-something or other. Highly poisonous but
a dead cert.' He produced a glass tube containing a small evil-
looking brown bottle. 'Next weekend we'll try it . . . .'

Next weekend was hot and sticky as usual that summer. We
entered a pinewood, roaring and metallescent as Kennedy Field.
We stopped. The Doctor went ahead. He selected a long pole from
the thinnings. He donned surgical gloves, then extracted his tube
from the rucksack, very carefully slid out the bottle, and loosened
its stopper. Throttles were opened. He disappeared behind a
hurricane of wings, became a pillar of buzz. Then slowly, miracul-
ously, the pillar condensed into a ball and the ball raised itself above
him, far above, clustering on the end of the pole. He signalled us to
replace the bottle and its tube into his rucksack, then strode on
ahead, bearing the cloud of flies aloft. So we progressed, taking
turns to hold the pole, bringing its end cautiously near any head
visited by less perceptive Diptera. No vacuum cleaner could have
done the job better.

Indeed miraculous; if somewhat odd in appearance. We mounted
the plateau (it was the Gorms that weekend), and the air cleared.
We gingerly laid down the pole and bolted a hundred yards or so.
Only a distant revelling. We were safe.

'Marvellous stuff. Pity it's so poisonous. He only let it out
because I'm a quack. Seems it's a sure thing for the Third World
when the molecule's been tidied up a bit. Should get some here after
Devolution.'

Coming down that evening, along the other edge of the corrie,
was more difficult. No forest, no poles. We did not risk a long grass
stem. Suppose it bent . . . . Instead, whenever our individual clouds
became too irritating, the Doctor stopped and dabbed a boulder.
Then we each went and, holding our noses, laid heads as close to it
as possible, and so decanted our flies. Behind us, a powerful telescope
would have revealed a succession of curiously-vibrating tumuli.

Peace, peace. Sheer luxury of seeing and hearing again. Of
owning one's hair.

Then, just before entering the wood—and its convenience of
poles—disaster struck. The Doctor had been the last to exchange
flies with the local granite. In completing this transaction he had
knelt—on the bottle . . . .

A terrible cry. We looked round. An immense cloud, and out of
it the Doctor running as if for life. Without his breeches or his
rucksack.

When we had all run half a mile, he stopped.

'Damned good job I had on the old linen ones. Just ripped 'em off, pants and all, and legged it. Stuff hadn't soaked through.'

The rucksack had dropped on to the contaminated garments and, like them, would be unapproachable until wind and weather had done their work. The rucksack contained our few spare clothes, and the Doctor would have to remain breekless. He was fortunate in wearing a long tartan shirt. We made him wash thoroughly in the burn and the Apprentice lent him his belt. Tucked in suitably, the sark now resembled a kilt; on the short side, but adequate. The Doctor chose a comfortable tree-stump, after inspecting it for ants. We munched the Apprentice's emergency rations, moist from his pocket.

'I'll come back for the things tomorrow night. No-one'll nick 'em in that state. We'll just have to go cannily down to the car. Don't want to be picked up like this . . . . O damn these flies.'

Our descent became hilarious. Peering through my nimbus I saw the Doctor leaping hairily and bonily ahead, a swashbuckling figure fresh from Killiecrankie or, less improbably, Mons Graupius. We spurred him with Hampden cries. He responded with bursts of *Nicky Tams*.

The path passed Glendrumly Castle. We took that stretch cautiously. Young Glendrumly was a keen ornithologist and possessed a troop of bird-feeding aunts who regularly crumbed the turrets. Also he had an uncle who was a part-time lunatic and occasionally cantered about garbed as the Doctor was now. Every window might have been manned. The Doctor was so intent on watching the Castle that he failed to notice a litter of tourists lying exhausted on his right. They sat up in alarm as he fled. We explained we were from the Castle and hurried on.

Though unsettled by this episode and by the unexpectedly warm driving seat, the Doctor relaxed when his hands were on the wheel.

'We'll go through Balqueenie. Some shops might still be open. Souvenirs and stuff. Might get shorts. Or at least bathing trunks.' He brushed flies from the windscreen, and we drove away.

Balqueenie was crowded. The road before us vanished into heaving tweed. Of course, the Highland Games. Balqueenie, if not artistically the summit of such gatherings, is certainly the social peak. We sniffed. We were snobs. We each had our favourite Meeting, and it was not Balqueenie. The Apprentice had lost his voice for Bill Anderson the week before at the *aficionados'* gathering at Brig o' Dinnie. The Doctor, when subjecting us to an approximate *piobaireachd* outside his tent, was likely to explain he had just heard that particular interpretation at Lochboisdale or Portree. I myself had come second out of three in a race up the local ben at Strath Warsle—a race, it is true, disorganised at an early stage by the landing amongst the original leaders of a hammer, thrown somewhat inexpertly from elsewhere in the programme. Obviously, we were not Balqueenie men; and we enjoyed the Apprentice's graphic suppositions of the ancestry and habits of the more outrageously decorated members of its ecosystem—a regular *Tartanetum*. The gilt-edge of the crowd, in dreepy kilts and clutching equally unconvincing seven-foot-long polished cromags which kept banging into and interlocking with each other, was being continuously photographed—no doubt as Real Jocks—by the more jovial fraternity in T-shirts and paper streamers. Watching good-humouredly were the whiskied red-faced possessors of the more indigenous genes. Aye, bonnie Balqueenie.

The road cleared. The Main Square. We wound down the window a little. At one end stood a group whose prolonged mass-acre of the accepted European phonetic values reduced even the Apprentice to silence. They, the really Top People, were accompanied by spectacled gentlemen of eastern appearance, heavily decked in smiles and telescopic lenses. About them stood brow-mopping men whose minds had obviously recently been relieved—the organisers. One of the organisers appeared familiar; he occupied a gratifyingly lived-in kilt. His eye brightened when he saw us. The Club Treasurer, in fact.

'Jamieson!' exclaimed the Doctor. 'That's him. Just the man I had to see. I never sent him those subscriptions—after all I promised.'

We drew into the kerb.

'I must apologise. Won't take a minute. Frightful lapse.'

The Doctor seized the door handle and sprang out of the car. He remained—for a split-second—springing, hairy legs Nijinsky-like, horror on his face. He was of course still clad only in his shirt.

Before he touched ground the Apprentice's splitter-second reflex, so welcome to us on many another crux, had whipped a travelling rug out of the back seat and over his descending frame. The Doctor, no less quick on the uptake, swept it round him in an instant, straightened, and then strode majestically forward across the Forum, attired in a somewhat dusty but nevertheless imposing toga of Ancient MacQuarrie. Before he reached Jamieson's group, which had been struck to unaccustomed silence, he had rustled up an almost believable Inverness cape. His breezy address prevailed and we watched, fascinated, as the eyes of Jamieson's companions slowly rose from the long folds of MacQuarrie to the animated bony countenance. Jamieson himself supported the Doctor manfully, though his bonhomie appeared of the anxious kind. The Doctor had no such inhibitions and seemed in great form, the Gentry rapidly responding with shouts of laughter and high whinnying dipthongs.

We trusted that our companion would remember to keep gestic-
ulating with his right hand and not with the left, which was
required for his rug.

The driver's window was darkened. Inspector McHaig. He
appeared subdued. He leaned heavily. We expected a cheerier
greeting. Perhaps he thought the Doctor had gone a little too far.
Drink and driving.

'Had a good day, lads?'

'Great. And how were the Games?'

'O fine, fine. Mr Jamieson's very pleased. And Royalty was
fair chuffed.'

'You look worried, Inspector. Don't mind the Doctor, he's . . . .'

'Aye, aye; but I'm afraid we've just had bad news . . . . There's
a body on the hill, lads.'

'Can we . . . ?'

'No, no. My chaps have gone up to bring it down.'

We'd thought we'd seen the Pitfoulie Land Rover trumpeting
and tusking its way through the throng earlier. 'Pitfoulie there as
well?'

McHaig darkened further. 'They've just rammed one of my
patrol cars. We've filled the ambulance already.'

'Helicopter?'

'Busy with the traffic. Anyway the poor felly'll not be needing
us to hurry, by all accounts.'

He looked meaningly at us. 'It's Captain Rawlings for sure,
I'm thinking.'

Captain Rawlings. That gentleman had provided the Pitfoulie
Mountain Rescue Team and its exuberant competitors with three
weeks invaluable heather-thrashing in the spring, before being
entered up finally as 'Not Found.' We had remained unsurprised
at this sad verdict. Captain Rawlings had been, it seemed, an
English visitor at the Inverfyvie Arms. He stayed a week. He was
popular with staff and guests. He was a willing, and successful,
hand at the cards. He stood generous drinks on account. And on
the Friday morning he had gone out—'for a walk on the hill.' He
would be back late that night.

He was not back late that night. Nor ever. *Cha till e tuille.* And
such a fine gentleman. Of course, very much a novice on the hill.
He had town shoes. Very inexperienced—why, he'd even carried
his suitcase, it seemed; for that, with his spare clothes, was missing
as well. And he'd made a careless mistake about his address, so his
next-of-kin—abroad, he had said—could not be traced. Tragic
indeed.

'Who told you it was Captain Rawlings?' we demanded.

The Inspector looked a little uncomfortable.

'Miss Threadweaver,' he said.

'Miss—?'

'She's staying at Glendrumly, helping with the junior bird-watching courses. Its Fledgling Week.'

'Did she *recognise* Captain Rawlings?'

The Inspector looked even more uncomfortable.

'Hout, no, man. Who could recognise him after all this time? And this hot weather. But she saw—A Heap, ye ken. Off the Creag Liath path.'

'But we've just come down the Creag Liath path and we've seen no Heap.'

'Well, she *did*,' said McHaig irritably, 'and she rang us up not ten minutes ago and I've sent men out there. She was all upset. Crying. She'd only bairns with her and darena get closer. "O, it's Captain Rawlings, Inspector," she said, "I know it is".'

'How *could* she know a heap was Captain Rawlings?' we persisted.

McHaig hemmed, and tapped the rim of the window. He gazed at the loquacious group across the Square, from which shrieks of well-dividended laughter could be heard. The Doctor's left hand was still firmly in place.

'There was claes and a rucksack.'

'But Captain Rawlings had a suitcase, not a rucksack.'

'He could have had a rucksack inside the suitcase and put it on when he got to the hill. Ye're better with a rucksack than a suitcase on a hill, are ye not?'

The logic was indisputable.

'Besides . . . .' A pause. 'It was not an ordinary heap of claes. There was an awful-like smell coming from it on the wind, if you understand me. And a great cloud of flies. Terrible lot of flies, she said.' He smacked the Triplex decisively. 'It'll be him, right enough. Three months, and weather like this. Poor felly. Anyway, my boys are up there, to bring him down, whoever he is. We've got to do it decently and quickly-like, with the Games on.'

The Apprentice and I looked at each other and swallowed hard. We leant over. We wound down the window to its fullest extent.

We began to explain.

ARRAN ODYSSEY

By W. M. M. Wallace

ODYSSEY: *A long wandering or a wandering tale*

No ONE would ever compare a traverse of the N.E. group of the Arran hills with that of the Cuillin main ridge. The latter is in an altogether different class as regards such factors as difficulty, physical and mental fitness, etc., whereas the former is, in comparison, little more than a long or relatively long, walk.

It is difficult to know how often the Arran traverse is done. It has never been the subject of any article or note in the *Journal*, nor as far as I know, in any other mountaineering journal, and indeed, almost the only comment I have ever read is that enigmatic sentence which appears regularly in each edition of the 'Islands' guide—quote—the entire main group of the Arran hills may be easily traversed in a long summer day.

Perhaps many people do it every year, but never feel it worth mentioning or recording. This seems unlikely when one considers some of the stuff actually recorded. More likely—few bother to do it at all—I don't know. Certainly, having traversed from Ben Nuis to Suidhe Fhearghas, and successfully reached the floor of Glen Sannox (as must be done by numerous climbers every year), it takes a certain masochism to then ascend the Cioch, and continue by the ridge via Goatfell to Brodick.

I made an attempt to do it on my own at Easter, about five years ago. I set off from my usual base in Brodick one morning at 9 a.m., climbed Goatfell, then made my way along the ridge to the Cioch. I descended into Glen Sannox then climbed up on to Suidhe Fhearghas, from which I followed the ridge south over the tops, reaching the Cir Mhor-A'Chir col at about 6 p.m. By this time I had run out of steam, food, motivation and almost everything else and in any case, it was going to be dark in two hours, and I was going to run out of daylight too. The decision was easy and I made it, returning home via Glen Rosa instead.

This attempt taught me two things. There was more to it than I had realised, and Easter was too early—at least for anyone moving at my pace.

During the next five years I continued to cherish the hope that I might yet do it, but they slipped by with no further attempt made. I should point out that this was no all-consuming passion (I was much too old for anything like that) but was more of a strong wish than anything else. I don't even know why I had such a wish—but

I had. Maybe I felt I'd done most other things in Arran, 'tho even that was by no means true.

The arrival of 1976 and the imminence of my 52nd birthday set me thinking again that I couldn't wait much longer, in case I got too old or dropped dead, or more likely Caledonia-McBrayne decided to blow the island up to save themselves further embarrassment.

I was of course, quite prepared to go alone, but did vaguely mention the project to a few other people, of whom only Hugh Stirling evinced even the slightest interest in joining me. However no plans were made and no time, other than a vague 'sometime this summer' suggested.

We met regularly, as has been our custom for years, about once a week, and during May and June even had a few evenings climbing at Loudoun. This again was the pattern of things, and did not represent even a gesture towards maintaining or attaining any semblance of fitness. The project was, for all practical purposes, forgotten in the meantime. Sometime during the second half of July, I don't remember the exact date, I went off to Arran for four weeks holiday with my family. Hugh had an open invitation to come down some weekend when the weather seemed reasonable, but nothing firmer was arranged. The weather was good during the first ten days, and I spent most of the time playing tennis or fishing. Only once did I go near the hills—a short day on the ridge from the Cioch to Goatfell.

On the second week-end of the holiday, Hugh suddenly arrived off the late Friday night boat. Carrying his usual two or three packs, he appeared at the cottage door and said 'Hullo. O.K. for tomorrow?'

'What about tomorrow?' I said, and the awful truth then dawned on me. This was it. He was expecting me to agree to attempt our traverse the next day. Thoroughly taken aback, I said 'Do you think we're fit enough?'

'No' he replied in his characteristic way, 'But if we wait till we are we'll never do it.' We had supper, washed down by a few drams, and during the course of what was left of the evening, it became increasingly clear that he really meant what he had said. The more I thought about the thing the more I too began to feel that the cavalier attitude was probably the right one, and that it really didn't do to indulge in too much thinking or planning. No one could have accused us of that. We had enough food, we didn't need to carry any water or gear, and the weather seemed suitable enough. We went to bed just after midnight, promising ourselves a 6 o'clock start.

We didn't quite make 6 o'clock, but left the cottage at 6.45 and drove to Davidson's Farm at the entrance to the lower part of Glen

Rosa. It was a dry day with broken cloud and a cool N.W. wind as we set off up the glen, making for the Ben Nuis path which follows the Garbh Allt burn and crosses the generally soggy Coire Bhradain to the S.E. shoulder of the mountain. Our pace was not fast but was very steady, and we reached the summit at 8.50 without a single stop, and thanks to the almost cold wind and our shorts, without breaking sweat.

After a short rest, we wandered along the broad grassy ridge to Ben Tarsuinn, the easiest part of the day, and thence down the rather ill-defined gravelly path to the so-called Bowman's Pass at the south end of A'Chir. Crossing the latter was especially familiar, but to me at least, is never boring. We omitted little and enjoyed the usual problems as much as ever although we didn't actually climb the summit boulder on this occasion—a gesture to energy conservation or something like that, I suppose. We took a short rest at the col north of the ridge, before making the rather dull ascent to the summit of Cir Mhor itself. By this time it must have been about 11.30 a.m. We were going quite well, and it was obvious that whatever else we ran out of, it wouldn't be time. The fresh north-westerly wind continued, and 'tho the day was bright, we were subjected to very little direct sunshine and were, consequently, able to remain well hydrated. The descent from Cir Mhor and the plod up Hunter's ridge to the Castles was duly accomplished with only the usual mandatory stop at the 'famous' springs for a drink. Water is rarely a problem on the Arran ridges, and one can usually find some somewhere. We reached the Castles' summit at about 12.30, and another little rest was taken. We were taking more rests now, but they were all short, and we remained in fairly good shape. It was here that Hugh said 'It's really a very photogenic day now. It's a good thing we didn't bring cameras. We'd never have made it.' On we went, scrambling along the ridge to the col at the Witch's Step, and up on to the latter's very small summit (the most difficult actual top in Arran) direct from the col. The final section of this part of the main ridge to Suidhe Fhearghas is easy walking, the sort of ground on which you can switch to 'automatic' if you're feeling a little tired. We reached Suidhe Fhearghas at about 2 p.m., and rested again. There are no comfortable ways off Suidhe Fhearghas. There are, of course, no technical difficulties, but any descent lies over very steep heathery boulder slopes, and no really good path exists. We decided to go back along the ridge a few hundred yards, to where the ground looked easier, and to go down from there. We planned to take this descent deliberately slowly in general to avoid undue jarring, and in particular to save Hugh's right knee. Something had happened to it a few years back, as the result of a ski-ing incident, and it tended to give him trouble at times. It had by now, begun to hurt, and my morale had sunk a little, when I saw him wrapping a crepe bandage round it, before beginning the descent to

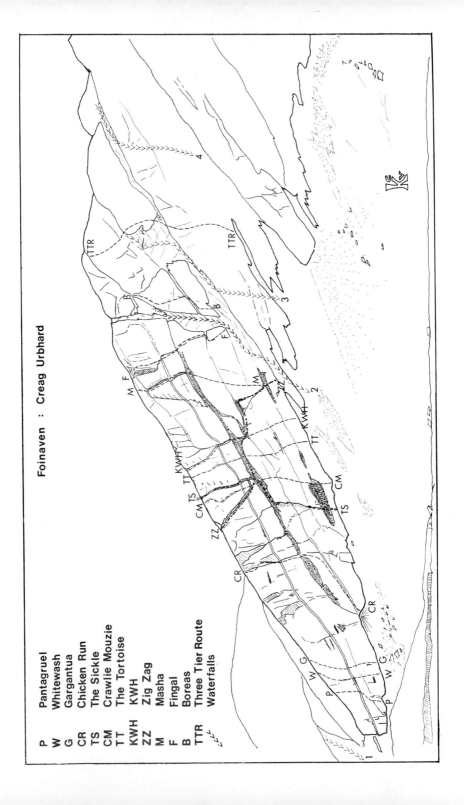

Foinaven : Creag Urbhard

P	Pantagruel
W	Whitewash
G	Gargantua
CR	Chicken Run
TS	The Sickle
CM	Crawlie Mouzie
TT	The Tortoise
KWH	KWH
ZZ	Zig Zag
M	Masha
F	Fingal
B	Boreas
TTR	Three Tier Route
⚡	Waterfalls

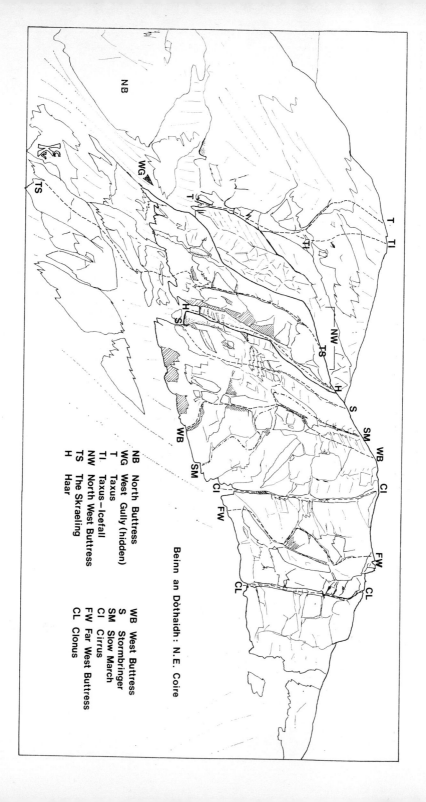

Beinn an Dòthaidh: N.E. Coire

NB	North Buttress
WG	West Gully (hidden)
T	Taxus
TI.	Taxus–Icefall
NW	North West Buttress
TS	The Skraeling
H	Haar

WB	West Buttress
S	Stormbringer
CI	Cirrus
SM	Slow March
FW	Far West Buttress
CL	Clonus

the glen. We reached the Sannox burn at 3 o'clock, and here we had our first and only long rest.

It coincided with about the only warm sunshine we enjoyed all day, and this contributed much to a most pleasant interlude. We just sat by the burn, our backs to the Cioch (this was probably deliberate but we were not conscious of this at the time), eating a little, drinking a little, smoking a little, and generally relaxing.

'How's the knee, Hugh?' I said 'No worse' was the reply.

'There's no path from here to the Cioch, you know' I went on, jerking my thumb over my shoulder at the mountain behind. 'We'll just have to plod up through the heather, and make for the left sky-line. We should reach the tourist path up there somewhere.' The conversation was desultory—restricted to brief interruptions of what was a companionable silence.

'All right' said Hugh at last, 'Are you ready?' That's exactly how it happened. No discussion. Nothing. Just a mutual tacit recognition that we would go on. Neither of us had apparently even considered giving up.

We left our little resting-place regretfully at 3.45, and set off towards the Cioch, which towered nearly 2,000 ft. above us. This was the crunch now—without a doubt. The going was hard, and with no path, every step meant raising tired feet completely clear of the tenacious heather. It was hard all right, but somehow not too hard, and we were tiring, but were by no means exhausted. A long time seemed to pass, however, before we eventually struck the upper reaches of the Cioch tourist path. The latter, like certain other tourist paths I know, must in places, pose problems for some tourists, particularly in the wet. On this occasion however, it meant for us only easier going, and at 5.30 we arrived on the Cioch, one of the finest summits in Arran.

We rested once more, but only briefly, before setting off on the penultimate lap of our mini-marathon. We were going slowly now, but still surprisingly steadily and still interested enough to take in all the tops, including even all the little rocky tors on the Stacach ridge between the two Goatfells. At about 7 p.m. we stood on the top of Goatfell.

We had done what we had set out to do, and although tired, felt thoroughly satisfied with our expedition.

'Nuis looks awful far away, doesn't it?' I said.

'Aye. It does.' replied Hugh. 'Especially the way we came.' We sat down to finish off the food. This wasn't difficult because there wasn't much left—indeed there hadn't been all that much to begin with. We have always tended to travel light—sometimes too light.

The last lap took us two hours, and it was 9 o'clock before we reached the cottage and staggered in, to be greeted by the usual 'Well? Good day?' from my wife. 'Are you hungry? Food'll be ready soon.'

It had been a good day, a very good day, all eighteen miles, eight thousand feet and fourteen hours of it, and one we would remember for a long time.

'We'll maybe do it again sometime when we're fit' was Hugh's final comment.

CREAG URBHARD

By Peter F. Macdonald

To WRITE about one particular crag in the Reay Forest, where rocks abound on every hillside, seems a trivial and almost pointless exercise. But Creag Urbhard is due an article, not only because it is the biggest and most unusual of them, but because its climbing routes have become more and more confused over recent years. Here more than anywhere else, we have seen bewildering reports of routes which are '*probably* to the left of Route X', or '*roughly* up the centre of the large buttress' and so on. One recent climb was even described by its author as 'impossible to describe'! It is unlikely that any one person has climbed even half of the routes so far existing and most of the available information is, at best, second-hand, so that one thinks twice before putting pen to paper. If this survey goes some way towards sorting out the muddle, rather than merely adding to it, then it will achieve its main object.

Creag Urbhard dominates the upper part of Strath Dionard, a desolate glen running north-westwards towards Cape Wrath. Together with the five Dionard Buttresses and Creag Alasdair it forms the east face of Creag Dionard, which is the south-most top of Foinaven. If you take the idyllic approach from the east by Strabeg, which you should not miss doing, you will be confronted on the Bealach na h-Imrich by this panorama of cliffs, with the grey ridges of Foinaven stretching out behind into the distance. Immediately opposite you, on the far side of Loch Dionard, is the great, sprawling mass of Creag Urbhard; but it is not until you are down beneath it that its true size and complexity become apparent. It is, in fact, a good thousand feet at its highest point and not far short of a mile from end to end.

The rock is quartzite, varying considerably in quality but often demanding extreme care, especially in its present, unfrequented state. Belays, even with pitons, can be difficult to obtain and this, together with the sheer scale of the place, makes every climb a serious undertaking. The general stratification, which is very prominent, runs from bottom left to top right. There are several waterfalls which help to identify some of the features but of course, their size and number vary according to the season and this has been one of the sources of confusion in the past. In the *Foinaven Supplement*[1] of 1966 Park and Tranter gave numbers to the four main waterfalls and these are now generally accepted. The First Waterfall defines the left-hand end of Creag Urbhard, separating it from the loaf-shaped First Dionard Buttress. To the right of this the crag rears up in a slightly concave lay-out, with a small, hanging corrie high up at the back. This corrie is drained by the Second Waterfall. The main feature of the cliff is the enormous face of the South Ridge which runs obliquely between these First and Second Waterfalls and it is here that most of the climbing routes lie; the face is split by a terrace at mid-height, with few features in the lower half but a series of fine, slanting dièdres above. About half way along the face, one of these dièdres combines with the edge of a rounded bastion in the lower tier to form a feature known as The Sickle. To the right of the Second Waterfall are the less continuous rocks of the so-called Central Buttress, across the lower part of which there runs a remarkable, rocky shelf appropriately known as The Pavement (or Lower Pavement). Onto this the Third Waterfall cascades from a fierce set of overhangs. To the right of this again, the Fourth Waterfall runs down a more broken part of the face and beyond that, the North Ridge stands out in a massive triangle with spectacular, twisted rock strata.

As on so many other Scottish crags, history began here with Ling and Glover, who in May 1910, ascended 'the skyline rising immediately from the top end of Loch Dionard.' This has been taken to mean the crest of the South Ridge, although according to their account and photographs they may well have started up the far side of what we now call the First Dionard Buttress.

> 'At first we had ledges of heather with faces of rock between them. Later the heather died out, and we had either bare steep rocks or sloping slabs with cracks and hollows which just held the side-nails. We could have made the route easier by going to the left, but we wished to keep as direct a line as possible. The leading was divided, Glover's turn giving him a fine run out on rocks rivalling the Dolomites for steepness. Higher up the angle eased, and after an hour-and-a-half's climbing we reached the top of the buttress 900 feet from the start.'[2]

Whatever their precise route, this was certainly a remote and adventurous outing for its period. No other climbs were recorded until 1950, when Parker and Young took a walk along the Lower Pavement—alias *Original Route, Central Buttress*—an easy but interesting way up the face. Then in 1951 and 1954, three routes were climbed by Tom Weir, Len Lovat and A. D. S. MacPherson in various combinations. These were the *North Face Gully* (in fact the Fourth Waterfall—'a good route for a foul day'!); the *Right-hand Route* of Central Buttress, on the rocks above the top end of the Lower Pavement; and the 1,000-foot *North Ridge*.

1959 saw the first two climbs on the South Ridge, both done by Terry Sullivan of the R.A.F., apparently on the same day but with different companions. These routes, *Pantagruel* and *Gargantua*, are on the white wall at the extreme left-hand end of the crag but are hard to locate exactly owing to the lack of features thereabouts. The easiest line on the South Ridge, *Zig-Zag*, was discovered by Neville Drasdo and Mike Dixon on a date which has gone unrecorded; very probably it was during the spring of 1962, when the same party made their more celebrated climb on The Fiddler of Ben More Coigach. Starting some distance to the left of the Second Waterfall, *Zig-Zag* follows a line of weakness slanting up leftwards onto the half-way terrace, which it then descends to gain an easy dièdre, also slanting to the left. Despite its wandering line, or perhaps because of it, this route provides a very rewarding expedition at a hard Difficult standard.

Then in June 1962 came Tom Patey, inevitably solo and equally inevitably, taking one of the most obvious lines. For all that, it is a line which presents route-finding problems and he gave it quite a detailed description. The route, *Fingal*, starts at the foot of the Second Waterfall and follows a line of cracks on the left wall, diverging gradually from the waterfall and continuing up the right-hand edge of a V-shaped depression in the top tier. In common with most of the climbs on the South Ridge, this gives about 900 feet of climbing of up to Severe standard and is a fine, mountaineering route.

The next developments came in 1965 when two ascents were made by members of the Corriemulzie Mountaineering Club. *Chicken Run*, climbed by Ian Rowe and Philip Tranter, takes the big, left-hand dièdre on the South Ridge, entering it by a rising traverse from the left and finishing with the hardest pitch in the final chimney. This is another very good line and in fact this and *Fingal* are the only two natural lines which run the full height of the South Ridge. *Boreas*, climbed the same day by Park and Macdonald, ascends the less difficult rocks immediately to the right of the Second Waterfall, to finish on an Upper Pavement beneath the still virgin walls of the hanging corrie.

The Squirrels were next to make their mark and in the two succeeding summers they disposed of two more features on the

South Ridge. In 1966, Bugs McKeith and Mike Galbraith visited the furthest right of the principal dièdres, but finding it full of vegetation they took to the clean, exposed arête on its left. Their only comment on the route, 'Kilroy Was Here!' was promptly abbreviated to *K.W.H.* and as the *Supplement* was about to go to press, there was no time to think of anything better. Route-naming went a stage further out of hand the following year when Dave Bathgate and Willie Pryde went and called their line *Crawlie Mouzie*! This ascent started off in the direction of the Sickle Handle, which again turned out to be a deep, vegetated cleft and so the party *crawled* out leftwards (no doubt on their hands and knees) into a smaller dièdre where the climbing was on rock. Both these routes must be open to variation in the lower tier but their upper pitches look good.

The Inverness Mountaineering Club were also active in 1967 and two climbs were recorded by their members, apparently in the area of Central Buttress. At least one of these seems to have been original but the descriptions supplied[3] are unfortunately too vague for identification. (At the risk of creating greater confusion . . . . they probably lie between the Second and Third Waterfalls). In 1968 the MacInneses added *Three Tier Route*,[4] which takes in about as much of Central Buttress as is possible, starting at the bottom of the Fourth Waterfall and finishing near the top of the Third, crossing the Lower Pavement *en route*. This climb comes in at GRADE IV, for those who understand numerical gradings.

The latest stage began in 1969 with a series of annual Sassenach raids which are still continuing. During this period a host of fine routes have been put up all over the Foinaven region, mainly by climbers from the Sheffield area. These climbs have tended to be called after the nick-names of their perpetrators, thus evading the S.M.C's official ban on eponymous nomenclature. Paul Nunn and Clive Rowland, two of the ringleaders, scored an early success with *Tortoise* (named after Rowland) which takes the front of the attractive, tapering buttress between *K.W.H.* and the Sickle Handle. This is obviously as good a route as any on Creag Urbhard. During the same visit another long route was climbed by Messrs. A. Howard and P. Phipps, *The Veterans*; their equally long description tells almost everything about the climb except where it goes, but it is evidently not far to the left of *Fingal* and it makes use of a chimney 'clearly seen from the ground as a moon-shaped crack.' In 1972 Clive Rowland and Dave Marshall produced yet another fine climb, starting at the foot of *Zig-Zag* and going directly up the crag by way of a huge, 110-foot corner. This corner runs immediately to the right of a thin buttress which is the main feature of the upper tier between *Fingal* and *K.W.H.* The route, *Masha* (after Marshall) is notable as the first reported V.S. on the face, though *Tortoise* may well be under-graded at Hard Severe.

Another recent climb which deserves a mention was made by C. Ogilvie and M. Searle in 1975. This one starts between *Fingal* and *Masha*, joins *Fingal* on the mid-way terrace and then follows that route for a short distance before traversing right to gain another upward line. There are two parallel crack-lines in this most inaccessible part of the upper crag and the route probably uses one of these: future historians should look for a peg which the party say they left at their penultimate stance. They named the route *Promiscuous Wall* on account of its loose character.[5]

Finally, last summer the Glaswegians Dunn and Paul added their contribution with *Whitewash*, a 550-foot V.S. on the wall between *Pantagruel* and *Gargantua*.

There are still enormous areas of unclimbed rock and though most of the important features have now been explored, even on these it is unlikely that two parties will follow quite the same route. The crag remains ideal for random mountaineering, selecting some general line and then picking one's own way up the innumerable corners, buttresses and open faces. Despite its late development, its character is not that of a modern crag and it is noted not so much for its fearsome steepness (though it does not lack this) as for its scale, atmosphere and route-finding interest. Foinaven is richly endowed with high-quality climbing crags, but Creag Urbhard is undoubtedly the Big Wall of the area.

References:

1. Supplement to the *Interim Guide to Easter Ross*, published by the Corriemulzie Mountaineering Club (now out of print).
2. *S.M.C.J.*, xi, 1911, 189-190.
3. *Inverness Mountaineering Club Magazine*, 1968, 21-22.
4. H. MacInnes, *Scottish Climbs*, Volume 2, 173.
5. Taken from an unpublished latter to the *Journal* Editor (1976).

Notes:

(i)   All routes mentioned have been more fully described either under the above references or in the *Journal*.

(ii) The un-named route and the route *Hobbit* reported in *S.M.C.J.* xxviii, 1966, 215-216 appear to have been repeat ascents of *Original Route* (Central Buttress) and the *North Ridge* respectively, or very close to them. The route *Mayday*, reported at the same reference, is probably on one of the Dionard Buttresses.

(iii) *Tortoise* is to the right of *Crawlie Mouzie* the whole way and does not start to the left of it as originally described (see *S.M.C.J.* xxix, 1971, 406).

(iv) In the photograph on page 169 of MacInnes's *Scottish Climbs*, Volume 2, the line shown for *K.W.H.* is in fact that of *Chicken Run*; the line shown for *Chicken Run* is not a route at all; the line shown for *Crawlie Mouzie* is approximately that of *K.W.H.*; *Crawlie Mouzie* itself is not marked; and the line shown for *Fingal* is much too far to the left.

J.M.C.S.—THE HISTORIES

Last year's Editorial jibes have borne fruit and we conclude our *Journal* celebration of the J.M.C.S. Golden Jubilee with the historical accounts of the Lochaber and London Sections. We look forward to the next instalments in say, 2000 A.D., if not before.

J.M.C.S.—LOCHABER SECTION

The Young Thirty-Year Old, 1945-75

By Jim Ness

THIRTY years ago my mother baked every Friday afternoon and in the evening the lads came round to scoff the lot whilst discussing climbing prospects for the week-end. Nowadays I brew beer myself and the Committee calls every five weeks with the same locust-like effect. It may or may not be significant but Lochaber has nearly twice as many office bearers as the other sections and they ALWAYS turn up for committee meetings. It was at the last such meeting that Houlker announced tersely into his glass 'Next .... a letter from Brooker .... wants a short history of the Section for the S.M.C. *Journal* .... O.K. for you Dad.' Grunts of approval echo from a dozen other glasses as that bunch of reluctant scribes unanimously agree to pass the buck. So, here I sit surrounded by old notebooks, old diaries, old letters and old *Journals*, wading in a sea of nostalgia and getting nowhere fast. A couple of years ago Paul Biggin, then editor of our Section Journal requested me to produce just such an article for the edification of the newer and younger members. Thinking that they were likely to learn little but nasty habits, I declined, but in place thereof wrote a short essay on the atmosphere and style of climbing at the time the Section came into being. Having declined too on the grounds that a History would merely be a catalogue of long gone names and exploits, I was surprised to find how almost Victorian was our outlook in the forties. It seemed to me too that those past expeditions would pale to insignificance beside the feats of modern tyros. In this latter however, it appears, on further questioning, the young hard men almost universally respect and admire the pathfinders and are well aware of the contribution which the J.M.C.S. has made to Scottish mountaineering.

When account is taken of the pre-war histories of the other sections Lochaber is the youngest, yet it is unique and integrated in a most important way—it is the only section actually based in a mountaineering area and consequently many inter-section friendships have built up simply because you cannot climb on Nevis or the Mamores without, as it were, stomping through Lochaber territory. Thus grew up in the early days a cross-flow of information, particularly regarding climbing partners and snow conditions. Further interchange resulted from the northward trek of all the southern worthies to climb, wine, dine and show their slides (or lantern lecture) and so it was we came to know the irrepressible Hamish Hamilton, MacKellar, MacPhee, Scott, Weir, MacKinnon, Humble and Murray. In fact all the names recounted by other section historians weave their way through Lochaber life and leave their mark.

The second half of the forties marked the exploration of Polldubh and the great Southern gullies of Nevis, of which the greatest, Strawberry Chasm, was later to be renamed Surgeon's Gully after Donald Duff, its most persistent adversary. Donald Duff had a tremendous influence in Lochaber; he had an indefinable integrity, an infectious enthusiasm and a gentle modesty which one rarely encounters these days. The Lochaber Section and modern mountain rescue organisation owe a great deal to him, as indeed do all of us who were young when he was in middle age. His sternest rebuke was once to press upon me, without further comment, a small envelope containing three or four Tricouni nails—these were clearly intended to replace the serrationless toe brackets I'd used when climbing with him a day or two before.

The acquisition of Steall Hut brought one of the finest mountain groups in Scotland, the Mamores, within easy reach. Alex MacKellaig was the first of many able and diligent Hut Custodians whose example spurred us all to give of our time and energy in restoration and bridge building—activities which proved to create a unity which other sections achieved through bus-meets. Right into the early fifties I spent many happy days working at Steall and climbing outcrops in the Mamores, in the company of that great club character, Jimmy Wyne. Raconteur superlative, he was invariably attired in a boiler suit and a two-day growth. A friend of Nimlin, he had an endless stock of tales about the escapades of Lomonds and Creag Dhu during the Depression. In winter Jimmy claimed his leaning was to good clean rock and in summer he relied on poor memories to expostulate his penchant for steep ice. This philosophy was a good let-out for us all on occasion in Lochaber but caused havoc if not hilarity on our first Alpine meet. He loved high camping in winter (genuinely) and always carried his harmonica and a set of 'pokey die'; with the former he entertained in the Arctic Guinea and with the latter he won all spare food and other goodies which could not be divided. Burgon and Corson completed the high camping foursome but the gates of Hell would have had to freeze before Bob Corson expanded on his standard 'No Bad' rejoinder to any enquiry about conditions of difficulty. On account of his ability to withstand great heat Jimmy was sometimes known as the Asbestos Wonder. He used this faculty to great advantage when wishing to acquire the best seat by a howff fire—he simply stoked up until the resulting inferno forced the rest to give way and by the time if had subsided Jimmy was ensconsed in the place of his choosing.

The man who did most to bring Lochaber within the J.M.C.S. fold was W. S. Thomson. Bill had the Glasgow 'connection' and he was an extremely competent all-round mountaineer who like Duff did much to encourage the younger members. Sadly Bill Thomson is no longer with us but his pictures live on and an era of Scottish mountaineering literature is enhanced by his compositions.

By the end of the forties Vibram soles were making their invidious entry but the change in style required was assisted by the arrival in Lochaber of climbers like Miles Hutchison, Stan Thompson, and Trevor Ransley. How far the Ben influenced the decision to advance their careers at British Aluminium, Fort William, only they can say but what is certain is that they lost no time in seeking out the Brotherhood. They brought a new polish and sophistication to our climbing; their sartorial elegance caused us passing shame if little noteworthy improvement—their friendship remains forever. Many of the more obscure buttresses and gullies previously dominated by the North Face had now been explored and Paddy Heron was at the height of his barn-storming Munro bashing. Paddy must be one of the few, if not the only person, to complete the 'Three Peaks' trip by driving the entire way there and back. Five of us went on that 24-hour jaunt round Nevis, Scafell Pike and Snowdon and it was not an experience I would care to repeat.

Looking back through the mists of time what appeared to be a descent of the Cresta Run turns out to be a vision of John Musto roaring through the 'Coe' on a freezing moonlight night, snow banked deeply on both sides and equal depths of Lochaberites standing charioteerlike in dicky and other superstructures, exhorting him to greater speed in his open tourer of obscure continental origin. It seems to have been getting warmer these last few decades for one never sees snow like that in the 'Coe' anymore, nor can you have an interesting afternoon's ice work in Achintee Gully.

Through the latter fifties and into the sixties the first young crop grew older and the inevitable drift from the Highlands in search of work took its toll. Miles Hutchison and others like Bill Robertson took the helm and steered the Club through this difficult time until the new crop fostered by Vic Quirie, Arthur Hill and Keith Stanley was ready to take the stage. Ian (Suds) Sutherland was one of the new local men. Suds, with his quiet manner and twinkling eyes, reminds me a lot of Donald Duff, a comparison not lightly made.

However, I recall no reluctance to drive with Duff and it was usually quite safe to be in the same room with him at a club or rescue team 'do.' On the other hand, I know no other who has turned down a gallantry award in favour of his comrades. Lochaber being one of the main exercise and 'action' areas, R.A.F. rescue men became quite well known locally and the number who have settled here has grown steadily over the years: one such being Ian (Spike) Sykes. Spike got Nevisport going on his return from the Antarctic and so we gained a climber of considerable stature, a gear shop, a central meeting place and a terrifying driver. Spike, they say around Lochaber, doesn't drive a car—he aims it.

Of all the migratory movements to affect mountaineering in Lochaber probably the greatest impact was from the arrival in Fort William of Scottish Pulp and Paper. This institution, it would seem, recruited an army of mountain men and billeted them *en masse* in our patch. The cohorts contained such men as Sandy Kane, already our Past President; Neil Parrish, the present Hut Custodian; the indefatigable Donald Watt and the irredeemable Willie Anderson. Alex Gillespie has forsaken paper for 'gear,' but his contribution to local climbing has only been enhanced by his joining the Nevisport Trio. The new era climbing demonstrated by John Grieve has come a long way and we now have very much more than a nucleus who not only can go anywhere, any time, but frequently do, and sometimes through rescue work, HAVE to. Come the summer again, we'll all be following Hitch and Houlker out to Polldubh for a limber up in the soft tropical Lochaber evenings, to fit ourselves with a bit of luck for bigger things at the weekend. Fordy won't be wearing his crash lid 'cos he can't remove his existing headgear, and Howie led by Shane will be there too, as usual, testing our rope and restraint to destruction.

No history of Lochaber would be complete without a more than passing reference to Mountain Rescue and whilst the Team nowadays is separate from the Club it is entirely manned by Club members. There are few countries in the world where rescue is a free operation by voluntary climbers and it is therefore a little disappointing on occasion to read snide comment, even in this august *Journal*, about the presence of teams in our hills. All casualties I ever met were grateful for the service and those who made no comment were never in a condition to make any. Lochaber men are frequently called to serve immediately upon return from their own expeditions and with the sophistication of modern climbing techniques, recovery often requires the highest degree of skill and endurance—Willie A after rescuing the same chap twice was reported to have said 'We'll have to stop meeting like this.'

Will Adam is our President this year, an office well deserved after nearly a decade as Treasurer. He reigns at one of the brightest periods in the history of the Club—may it always be so.

J.M.C.S.—LONDON SECTION

(1) The Early Days

By Hugh Jordan

THE ENGLISH connection with the J.M.C.S. was born in March 1939. What was formed was not a section in its own right but a London Association. Most of the founder members are now just names in an immaculately kept accounts book, but they include Zenthon, Pyatt and Folkard, names that are still meaningful in the Section. There could hardly have been a more unfavourable year to form a climbing association. One year later a hurredly written circular stated 'organised activity is now impossible and the distribution of meets details can serve no useful purpose.' It then gave a list of members likely to climb who were on leave in the South East. The circular was too pessimistic and climbing not only continued, but appears to have increased. The concentration of climbers in the London area and the services of the London Association as a clearing house, made its own peculiar wartime contribution to the development of the Sandstone Outcrops. The latter development was to earn a reputation for the London J.M.C.S. and it was Ted Zenthon who pioneered much of this work. Archives contain impressive accounts of bivouacs at High Rocks to make sketch maps whilst the bombs fell nearby.

Activity was by no means limited to the South East. Zenthon made a visit to Glencoe when contact was made with Bill Murray. This was not their first meeting however and a friendly link developed which was to prove invaluable in years to come. Other activities included a convalescence meet in the Lakes and visits to Bethesda in 1944. If it was Zenthon who was the principle founder of the Association, then it was Ted Pyatt who steered the negotiations through difficult Northern waters, which resulted in the formation of our Section. Shortly after the end of the war Zenthon went to Scotland hoping for support to establish the new Section. No encouragement came his way. Murray nevertheless wrote to Pyatt urging him to press on with the matter and take it to the A.G.M. 'In an A.G.M. you find none of that narrow nationalism that sometimes appears in area committees.' The main opponent was one named Drummond Henderson who in the same correspondence to Pyatt was dismissed as a 'rabid nationalist who represented a very small minority of vociferous Scotsmen.' Murray proved to be right and with Pyatt as Secretary and Zenthon as President, the J.M.C.S. London Section came into existence on the 1st of January 1946.

The Section had dual functions. It served the needs of southern-based climbers and continued to establish itself as the authority on Sandstone climbing in the South East. Ted Pyatt published the first guide in 1947, little more than a year after the official birth of the Section. In that same year its expertise was used by the C.C.P.R. in guiding groups of national officials around the outcrops. However the Section was keenly aware of its Scottish origins and several meets were held there each year. In an accident on the Ben in 1953, Peter Drummond Smith and David Monroe were killed. The parents wished to open a memorial hut and obtained a lease on Linneraineach at Coigach in Wester Ross. This was only to be a temporary measure until a permanent hut was built at Coruisk. As a result Linneraineach became the London Section's Hut. There followed a rapid development of climbs in the Stac Poly area. It had much to offer and J. H. B. Bell, after staying there in 1958, wrote to London advising an itinerary for climbing at Coigach. His own ascents in the area are to be found in *S.M.C.J.*, 1959, *XXVI*. The lease was but temporary and in 1959 Linneraineach passed back to the Inverpolly Estate and was lost to climbers. Although well served by its custodian, Ken Cox, the Section soon experienced the difficulties associated with a hut 600 miles away. The goods and chattels were stored in the old school at Inverpolly until evicted from there into a byre. Cox, who was working on the west coast, combed the neighbourhood for likely properties since the Section was keen to maintain its connection with Coigach. After two years of fruitless search the net was widened and came very close to success. An attempt at leasing the old school house at upper Glendessary, at the head of Loch Arkaig was made and fell through only at the last moment.

By this time the Section was well established and climbing regularly in mountain areas, in fact more so than on the sandstone outcrops. It became one of the best customers of the infamous Roy Cork coach which on Friday evenings before the days of the M1, chugged its way from Waterloo station (7 p.m.) to arrive at Idwal in Snowdonia next morning (4 a.m.) and make the return journey within 36 hours. The Section was becoming an English club with centres in Manchester, the North East and Nottingham. From the last named the Section's current Hon. President, now a distinguished and responsible statesman of mountaineering, regularly burned a dangerous passage through the night to Wales on a famous motor bike. The motorway was built and Bill Wallace moved to London for a while. The Slow Coach gave way to an alarmingly quick mode of transport, namely the Wallace Hire Van. Wales was becoming a major attraction and the influx of new members which was about to take place saw more logic in having a club hut in North Wales. This was a heresy to some founder members and marks a watershed of emphasis within the Section.

(2) The Last Ten Years

By John Steele

WITH THE acquisition of a club cottage in North Wales in 1964, the Section changed quite dramatically. The 'old guard' very quickly disintegrated, the remainder however, including Joe Della Porta, soon took advantage of the opportunity to introduce new blood into the Section. Activity took off and members such as John Wurflinger and Geoff Cohen were regular visitors. Naturally most weekends were spent in Wales, although the traditional New Year meet continued. An enthusiastic group from Birmingham had grown in a few years only to be rivalled by a hard climbing and ribald crew from Leeds, then Manchester and Liverpool, with always the London faction forming the predominant core. Typical of this period was a day on the hill followed by memorable drinking and singing sessions which lasted well into the night. (How we have changed in a decade!). It was a time when each visit to the hut would bring contact with another group of new people, hillwalkers and climbers alike. Everyone congregated at Glanafon at one time or another, therefore it was not long before a conversion programme was initiated. Changing No. 18 from an early 20th century dwelling house to a proper climbing hut was well advanced within a few years. Mass work weekends under the guidance of Tony Griffiths took place. His enthusiasm was infectious and many learnt the trades of demolition and reconstruction.

It was shortly before this time that I joined the London Section, having moved south from Scotland. Those early days on the west coast, mainly shared with my brother, Sandy, were for me the most important of all. Misty days on the Old Kilpatricks, trips to Arran, long treks in the Cairngorms, testing nerves on local quarries and the law on Dumbarton Rock and always Glencoe at New Year. So the Section had to contend with the two of us who even at that stage were determined to establish and keep a Scottish connection, intially because it was our natural feeling, but after a few years so that fellow travellers could maintain links with the J.M.C.S. while south of the border as we had been able to do. This Scottish identity has always been a problem, made more so by the fact that as the Section became larger and North Wales the centre of our activity, new members viewed us as an English club with little support for maintaining links with the other sections. Our belief has not been in vain however, as more recently a greater appreciation of Scottish mountaineering has developed in the Section, the increased awareness being reflected in the number of members climbing in Scotland throughout the year.

Given the natural tendency to look askance at anything of southern origin, particularly a body claiming national affiliation; the feeling of being merely tolerated by the rest of the Club has been prevalent over the years. So the London Section grew mostly in isolation but for the occasional meeting at whole Club functions. However, we have been able to maintain a fairly stable committee over the last ten years. This has helped enormously in establishing ourselves in England where the level of competition from other clubs is far greater than in Scotland, although in the East, particularly around Edinburgh, some similarity now exists. Thus much of our time has been spent in building up a club within England, hopefully without losing its Scottish flavour.

So the London Section in the early 1960's started afresh and, with a hut in North Wales, drew membership countrywide. That in essence is the Club's structure, but what of its content, its real purpose and its meaning in our lives? To answer these questions I personally do not have to look far. Under the guidance of a few older members, I soon decided that climbing to a higher standard each year was going to be a feature of my life. To this end Club meets became extremely important and other hobbies gradually fell by the wayside. Standards ranged from the pure hillwalker to the young tiger. It was easy to choose without pressure at which level you participated. The air of liberalism was as real in the Club ten or twelve years ago as it is today. Any cliques that existed were soon dispelled in the Douglas Arms on Saturday night so that you could find yourself on the end of a rope next morning grappling with some rain soaked Very Severe. Members such as Ron Yuen, Ralph Dickson (sadly lost shortly afterwards), Dick Lee and Bob Gray were the main perpetrators of such antisocial behaviour, but it was important in raising Club standards rather than erasing its members. There was a surprising intermix of climbing factions in the Section, most of us being teenagers under the loose leadership of a few more experienced members. Some traditional meets, such as Helyg, the camping meets at Cwm Silyn and in the Lake District, retained their popularity year after year. It was on these trips that most of us became proficient mountain campers, drinkers, and for the record, climbers. Therefore by the end of the sixties the bulk of the London Section, having joined as mere novices were becoming competent mountaineers in their own right. This led to a natural break-up, the Leeds group forming their own club, the Birmingham group moving into other activities and of course there was always the eternal scourge of all climbers, marriage. Activists such as Bill Humm, Pete Crewdson and many more were never to be seen again. Others spread their wings and left Britain: Graham Soar to the Antarctic and Maurice Grout to New Zealand, to name only two. Thus dozens of us spent most of the sixties in the London Section maturing from teenagers into men. I am sure that all those involved feel themselves fortunate to have been in a Club which tolerated and educated at a time when mass education without individualism was being advocated.

An influx of new members began in the early seventies. These were people who had previous club experience but liked what our Section had to offer. Friends such as Trevor Burrows, Andy Hughes and Peter Foster came and stayed and have subsequently progressed to Alpine climbing. Even more recently, experienced climbers like Peter Stokes and Leni Smith have joined, bringing a high standard of climbing into the Section.

For the future, the London J.M.C.S. is in good hands. With Hugh Jordan and Peter Whitechurch using all their mediatory skills, a balanced committee is assured. Bill Stephens is a godsend as far as hut works are concerned and the Club's climbing activity is now reaching as far as the Himalayas. I personally view the future favourably and can see our Section playing a role in mountaineering politics south of the border, while on a more savoury note, furthering the love of mountaineering in Scotland. May I say finally that those mentioned in this article are the names that first came to mind on particular points and that to include everyone, friends and acquaintances alike, would probably fill two chapters.

FOR AULD LANG SYNE

There's a ring about the mountains and the waters of the West,
Long, long ago it captured me, this land I love the best;
A legend so alluring and the glimpse which mem'ry frames
In my mind, as I'm recalling the magic of these names.

Imagination boggled when, in a day now long gone by,
I saw the gnarled outline of the Cobbler cross the sky;
'Can this be really true?' I thought, 'Such challenge to explore!'
The fates decreed I'd reach its top some fifty times and more.

The old road round Loch Tulla crosses high o'er Rannoch Moor,
I'll not forget that evening with its beckoning allure
Of Buachaille in the gloaming and the portal of Glencoe,
Bidean, Aonach Eagach, many more we came to know.

In course of time there came to us in days of rain and shine,
Mem'ries of a lifetime spent beyond the Highland Line;
Stob Gabhar and the Crowberry and Ben Nevis by the Tower,
Our lifting eyes to scan the hill gave grace to many an hour.

Go north by Ardnamurchan and you will surely come
To where the picture opens to the mountains over Rhum;
And yet that's but a preface for the searching eye that's keen
To catch on the horizon the far-off Cuillin scene.

O where can one appropriate in essence more sublime,
The spell that haunts the Highlands there, strong in the summer
                                                    time,
Than the ridge from Sgùrr nan Gillean and the thrilling galaxy—
Peak after peak to Garsven, sweeping downward to the sea.

———

The hills are higher now I think, than in those earlier days,
And loch and moor less reachable, as slower grow my ways;
Yet through the eye that lights the mind with vivid memories,
An 'after-glow' I still can know and see the Hebrides.

A.G.H.

NEW CLIMBS SECTION

GRADING POLICY. Aspersions have been cast northward suggesting that our reluctance to embrace the full range of fractured severity as practised south of the Border is an indication of hardening arteries, senility or even out-dated racial prejudice. Ever mindful of honest criticism we have searched our hearts, and even more important, consulted active climbing opinion on the matter. Views differ between those who would like to see standardisation with England and Wales—subdivisions of V.S. into all its subgrades and the adoption of individual pitch gradings, and those who wish to retain the simple Scottish V.S. in all its glorious ambiguity. Between lie the Majority who react favourably to the move made in our last issue to divide the highest grade into V.S. and H.V.S. categories, the latter including everything above V.S. We may well adopt an X.S. grade in the future, but this will be when there are more climbs—and climbers, in this category.

There is an immediate requirement to revise the grading of existing V.S· routes into the two sorts. A start has been made in the lists that follow. These cover some of the climbs in some of the major areas. There is a good deal of reassessment to be done and we would welcome opinion as to which category other existing V.S. routes should be assigned.

ROUTE NAMES. We note a recent inclination to submit unnamed routes· If a route is worth doing, then it is equally worth naming; we can supply names of our own but would prefer the originator's brand, provided of course these meet the minimal acceptable standards. (See *S.M.C.J.*, 1975, xxx, 383). If a route follows an identifiable feature then the name should include it. How many of us would wish to climb Clachaig Gully if it were called 'Yip-Yap' or something equally obscure and irrelevant? Again, a first winter ascent of an already named feature does not require an additional route name.

FIRST ASCENTS. The alphabetical rule for route-makers was suggested in the 1969 *Journal* and approved in 1970. We retain this, but where the information is available, propose to add the modification of a + sign for seconds who really come second.

Thus:—*I. Dangle and U. Whack* is the normal situation where the lead is shared.

—*I. Dangle + U. Whack* means that any actual dangling was done by Whack.

The system will even cater for the rope of three with a single leader—*A. Grunt + I. Dangle and U. Whack*, or with a leader at either end—*A. Grunt, U. Whack + I. Dangle*, where Dangle may well have lived up to his name.

CRAG REVISION. Financial restraints on the Rock Climbing Guidebook programme and other factors have made it increasingly difficult to maintain an up-to-date coverage of climbing crags. In this issue an article on Creag Urbhard, Foinaven, corrects the situation for that crag and also attempts to profile its character. We hope to continue this policy in future issues and welcome suggestions from contributors.

REVISED GRADINGS

Northern Highlands: Carnmore Crag

HARD VERY SEVERE

Abomination	Carnmore Corner	Penny Lane
Balaton	Dragon	St. George

VERY SEVERE

Black Mischief
Boo Boo
Connie Onnie
Fionn Buttress

Fionn Castle
Gob
Green Corner
Happy Wanderer

Original Route
Red Scar Entry
Tinkerbell

Cairngorms: The Loch Avon Horseshoe

HARD VERY SEVERE

Snipers
The Needle

The Pin
The Steeple

Thor

VERY SEVERE

Longbow Direct
Pushover

Python
Sandpyper

The Citadel
Whispers

Lochnagar

HARD VERY SEVERE

Crypt

Mort

Psyche

VERY SEVERE

Parallel B

Pinnacle Face

The Link

Creag an Dubh Loch

HARD VERY SEVERE

Cougar
Culloden
Dubh Loch Monster
Goliath

Gulliver
Predator
The Blue Max
The Giant

The Kraken
Vampire
Waterkelpie Direct

VERY SEVERE

Black Mamba
Cyclops
King Rat

Late Night Final
Mousetrap

Pink Elephant
Vertigo Wall

These climbs are *not* listed in order of difficulty.

Ben Nevis

HARD VERY SEVERE

Arthur
Brass Monkey
Centurion
King Kong

Knuckleduster
Shield Direct
Sioux Wall
Subtraction

The Bat
The Bullroar
The Crack
Torro

VERY SEVERE

Astronomy
Central Route
Minus One Direct

Minus Three Gully
Sassenach (slings)
Strident Edge

The Shield
Turkish

Glencoe I: Buachaille Etive Mór

HARD VERY SEVERE

Apocalypse
Apparition
Bloody Crack
Bluebell Grooves
Carnivore
Cayman Grooves
Dingle
Doom Arête
Gallows Route

Garrote
July Crack
Lecher's Direct
Le Monde
Line Up
Mainbrace Crack
Mainbrace Direct Finish
Nightmare Traverse
Pendulum

Plink
Pontoon
Shibboleth
Snowbas
Superstition
The Whip
White Wall Crack
Yam
Yamay

VERY SEVERE

August Crack	May Crack	Revelation
Bludger's Route	Neolith	South Chimney
Dwindle Wall	Paladin	of The Chasm
Flamingo	Peasant's Passage	The Mutchkin
Lift Off	Pirhana	The Widow
Limbo	Rannoch Traverse	Whispering Grooves
June Crack	Raven's Edge	Whortleberry Wall

Glencoe II: Bidean nam Bian

HARD VERY SEVERE

Girdle, N.F.A.D.	Marshall's Wall	The Duel
Hee Haw	Satyr	The Fly Man
Hesitation	Scausor	Trapeze
Kingpin	Stumblebum	Unicorn
Kneepad Direct	The Big Top	Yak
Kuf	The Cough	Yo Yo

VERY SEVERE

Agarophobia	Fingal's Chimney	Steptoe
Boomerang	Footpad	Stickleback
Central Grooves	Girdle, E.F.A.D.	Stook
Consolation	Kneepad	The Gut
Crow Step	Little Boomerang	Tober
Deep Gash Gully	Spider	Turnspit

Etive Slabs

HARD VERY SEVERE

Agony/Ecstasy	Long Wait	The Pause
Claw	Long Wait Direct Finish	The Pinch
Dan	Long Walk	Thin Red Line
Groundhog	Swastika Direct	Tous-les-deux
Jaywalk	The Band of Hope	
Long Reach	The Big Ride	

VERY SEVERE

Attila	Hammer	Swastika
Ba's	Sickle	The Grasshopper
Frustration	Spartan Slab	

Garbh Bheinn of Ardgour

HARD VERY SEVERE

Garnet	The Clasp	The Peeler
Sapphire		

VERY SEVERE

Cantata	Iubhair Groove	Scimitar
Drongo	March Buttress	Variation
Excalibur	Mournblade	(Shields, Route II)
Interrupted Slab	Outside Edge Route	

Southern Highlands: The Cobbler

HARD VERY SEVERE

Club Crack	Glueless Groove	The Nook
Dicer's Groove	Ithuriel's Wall	
Gladiator's Groove	MacLeans Folly	

VERY SEVERE

Cupid's Groove	Gimcrack	Whether Wall
Deadman's Groove	Gladiator's Groove Direct	
Direct Direct	S-Crack	

NEW CLIMBS — SKYE

Coire Na Creiche: Sgùrr a'Mhadaidh.—*Megaton.*

830 ft.   Hard Very Severe.

Pitches 1–3, C. Boulton, P. Nunn & R. Toogood. September 1972.

Pitches 3 on, M. Boysen, P. Braithwate & P. Nunn. April 1974.

The climb starts centrally, below the widest point in the overhangs; 250 ft. above and right of *Thor*. Climb lower slab to belay below overhangs (120 ft.). Traverse right to basalt breach in overhanging wall, climb to large ledge and belays (130 ft., escape possible). Gain upper slab, traverse horizontally to its lip, small stance and peg belay (80 ft.). Using combined tactics, gain and climb left slanting ramp, (peg runner in place) to small stance and peg belay (80 ft.). Climb up for 40 ft., traverse left to easier slabs (120 ft.). Continue more easily, finishing close to *Shining Cleft* on the rounded rib (300 ft.).

—*Quark.* 700 ft.   Hard Very Severe.

C. Boulton & P. Nunn. 28th August 1976.

Takes a direct and fierce line between *Thor* and *Megaton*. Start 90 ft. right of *Thor*. Climb slab to stance below steep wall (50 ft.). Climb groove on left past large poised blocks to vertical basalt dyke, move left and follow shallow fault to upper slab, go up left to good ledge, peg belay common with *Thor* (100 ft.). Go diagonally right to steep groove, climb 25 ft. to a standing place, poor protection. Using a very poor peg, (in place), traverse right to a small stance and belay (80 ft,). Climb hanging black groove (peg runner), to roof, traverse right, then up more easily on steep rock to the traverse line, move right to belay (70 ft.). Climb groove, move left to easier ledges then follow ramp back right (150 ft.). Continue more easily (250 ft.).

Coire a'Ghreadaidh—*North-West Ridge of Sgùrr a'Ghreadaidh*

M. Don & R. J. C. Robb. 10th December 1976.   1,000 ft.   Grade II.

An ascent under complete snow and ice conditions. Follow left flank of *Eagle's Gully* to its termination. Traverse up and left to gain a small ridge below the short, steep slab. Climb slab to crest of main ridge. The ridge is then followed to its junction with the west face of Ghreadaidh. Climb the face by steep shallow gully for 200 ft., then more easily to summit crestline.

Coire na Dorus: Sgùrr a'Ghreadaidh.

The following climbs lie on the buttress to the left of that which contains *Hamish's Chimney* and *Scimitar*:

—*Trapist.*   290 ft.   Very Severe.

G. Evans & J. Harwood. 3rd June 1976.

This follows the trap-dyke/crack at the left side of the buttress.

—*Simplicity.*   560 ft.   Severe.

G. Evans & J. Harwood. 3rd June 1976.

A pleasant route. Start below smooth-looking slabs towards the left side of the buttress. Follow trap-dyke up slabs then go rightwards to belay under large overhang (130 ft.). Climb overhang on right, continue easily up to grass ledge (120 ft.). Climb wall above (130 ft.). Scramble to base of final wall (100 ft.). Climb rough, juggy wall to top (80 ft.).

—Gauche.   490 ft.   Very Severe.
G. Evans & J. Harwood. 3rd June 1976.

Follows crack on right side of buttress. The second and fourth pitches are good, the latter taking an exposed arête between a chimney and grooves, and leading to the summit.

Coire 'A'Ghrunnda: Sgùrr Alasdair—*Sundance.*   250 ft.   Very Severe.
B. Dunn & A. Paul. 5th August 1976.

Start up overhanging recess immediately left of *Grand Dièdre*, exit out left. Trend up and right into small corner which is climbed to easier ground and belay (110 ft.). Climb steep slab above, split by crack higher, continue to ledge and belay (120 ft.). Climb up steeply on leftward slanting slab, move out right to gain arête and continue to top (80 ft.).

Marsco: North-West Buttress.—*Teflon.*   430 ft.   Very Severe.
G. Evans & J. Harwood. 1st June 1976.

This route lies on the same face as *The Boojum* (*S.M.C.J.*, 1969, xxix, 185). Start below and left of the cave. Scramble up to belay below buttress left of the cave (150 ft.). Climb buttress until possible to traverse down and right into cave, peg belay (140 ft.). Move out of cave and back onto lip (as for *The Boojum*), then go up to ledge (90 ft.). Continue to belay below final wall (110 ft.). Traverse left under overhang then climb to top (90 ft.).

NORTHERN HIGHLANDS I

Letterewe Forest: Beinn Airidh a'Charr: North-West Face.—*The Roc.*
M. Boysen, P. Braithwaite & P. Nunn. April 1974.   270 ft.   Very Severe.

Climbs the centre of the slabby face on the right flank of *The Beanstalk* arête. (*S.M.C.J.*, 1973, xxx, 168). Start 75 ft. right and up from *The Beanstalk*. Climb diagonally left up steep rock to overcome a lower bulge, traverse back right to belay below groove (130 ft.). Climb groove to stance on right (120 ft.). Finish up deep groove (50 ft.).

The Fannichs: An Coileachan: Garbh Coire.—*Beta Gully.*
C. Rowland & D. Scott. December 1976.   700 ft.   GRADE III.

Approaching from Fannich Dam, this is the second gully from the left. The first 300 ft. was interesting ice, followed by 400 ft. of easy snow.

Beinn Dearg: Inverlael Wall.—*Bonus.*   700 ft.   GRADE III.
A. McHardy & C. Rowland. January 1976.

Immediately right of Number 2 Gully is a diagonal snow slope, joining the gully at 300-400 ft. This route climbs the snow slope for 200 ft. then moves diagonally right to gain and climb a narrow gully.

NORTHERN HIGHLANDS II

Beinn Eighe: Coire Mhic Fhearchair: Far East Wall.—*Colgarra.*
R. Archbold & G. Cohen. 21st August 1976.   350 ft.   Hard Very Severe.

This very steep route starts centrally at a deep slit cave, between *Sundance* and *Kami-Kaze*. In its upper reaches it takes a hanging chimney, visible immediately right of a left curving groove. Climb left side of cave then diagonally left to grass ledge. Traverse right then go up past the horizontal fault into a groove; step right onto rib and so to belay at large jammed flake, visible from below. From just above belay swing right onto steep wall, go up flake crack to smaller flake. Climb 10 ft. of groove above then use slings for 15 ft. to reach good holds leading up and left to hanging chimney and grass ledge above. Climb up and left to small overhang, sling used to avoid loose block, follow crack to easier ground.

Eastern Ramparts.—*Shang-High.*

R. Archbold & G. Cohen. 20th August 1976.   440 ft.   Very Severe.

A feature of this route is the prominent chimney between the upper reaches of *Samurai* and *Gnome Wall.* Start about 40 ft. right of *Samurai,* just right of a detached pillar. Climb obvious crack line to grassy ledge 30 ft. below *Upper Girdle.* Go diagonally right onto huge flat-topped block, then up to *Upper Girdle*; climb crack for 20 ft., move right and up steep wall until able to move right to belay in the prominent chimney. Climb chimney to large slotted roof, turn this by crack on left. Continue steeply to top.

Central Buttress: Sandstone

Tier.—*Central Corner.*   230 ft.   Very Severe.

A. Nisbet & N. Spinks. September 1976.

Follows the very prominent dièdre on the left flank of the buttress, left of *Readymix* The route is easy for its grade but very sustained. Recommended. (A previous description of this section of cliff 'vertical for nearly 200 ft. with an overhanging base . . . .', appears to be somewhat hyperbolic).

Central Wall.—*Assegai.*

P. Baines & D. Nichols. 24th April 1976.   350 ft.   Very Severe.

Immediately right of *East Central Ribs* is a parallel rib, about 100 ft. high. Right of this again is a line of slanting, and steep narrow slabs, ending on the right at a prominent corner. Start on the broad terrace, 100 ft. left of the neck behind the *Tower.* Climb slabs to *Upper Girdle,* then groove on left to good stance. Traverse left then up, cross to stance. Climb straight up, strenuous, peg runner on left (crux), climb loose block into overhung chimney and stance. Follow chimney and go right to wall and stance on edge of precipice. Finish up wall of loose blocks.

West Buttress: Sandstone Tier.

Just left of the centre of this tier is a large, obvious corner. Left of this are two grooves; one on the lefthand side of the buttress overlooking *West Central Gully,* and the other midway between the central corner and the left edge of the buttress. The following three routes follow the two grooves and the corner, and are described from left to right. A fourth route is described last.

—*Sideshow.*

B. J. Chislett & R. A. McHardy. August 1976.   265 ft.   Very Severe.

On lefthand side of buttress overlooking *West Central Gully* an obvious groove runs almost to top of the tier. Start below and left of an obvious spike. Climb up and right past spike to groove, up this to overhang, turn this on the right and continue in same groove to ledge. Move up and right to large rock ledge below flared chimney. Climb chimney to grass ledge then take rocks above to easy ground.

—*Junior.*

R. A. McHardy & J. McLean. August 1976.   290 ft.   Hard Very Severe.

The groove midway between the central corner and the left edge of the buttress. The lower section is usually wet. Climb directly from the bottom to a large ledge on the left. Climb round cracked overhang above and follow grooves to a grass ledge. Continue to gain easy ground.

—*Senior.*

D. M. Jenkins & P. F. Macdonald. August 1976.   400 ft.   Hard Very Severe

The central corner. Start from grass terrace and climb direct throughout, taking the right-hand of two cracks at mid-height. Finish straight up quartz wall.

The fourth route lies about 50 f t. right of *Junior.*

—Relayer.

B. J. Chislett & R. A. McHardy. August 1976. 290 ft. Very Severe.

Climb easy groove to ledge and belay (30 ft.). Follow groove over small bulge to ledge, move up and right into small niche, traverse right to another small niche (peg runner). Climb to small overhang, traverse right, then back up left to foot of small prominent corner. Climb groove a few feet, go left along ledge. Move up over small bulge and right into short corner, climb this, rocks above to grass ledge, then obvious easy groove to reach easy ground.

West Buttress: East Face.

—Mistral. 400 ft. Very Severe.

B. J. Chislett & R. A. McHardy. August 1976.

The major feature is an obvious vee corner at the top right of the wall. The route leads fairly directly to the corner. Start from grass terrace at foot of wall, at an obvious groove (arrow). Climb groove to good ledge below overhang capped chimney. Climb wall right of chimney on good rock to reach wet crack, peg belay on left. Climb bulge, go right and up to small block overhang, step left onto nose and climb wall into groove above, belay below prominent corner first mentioned. Climb corner to top.

Liathach: Stuc a'Choire Dhuibh Bhig.—*Stringless Gully.*

500 ft. GRADE II.

A. Barney, P. Nunn, C. Rowland & R. Toogood. December 1976.

Directly above Choire Dhuibh car park and probably climbed previously. This is the first obvious line left of the Coire Dubh path and is a deep gully with steep side-walls. Two minor pitches.

Coire Dubh Beag.—*Footless Gully.* 500 ft. GRADE IV

C. Rowland + A. S. Rowland. February 1977.

Plainly seen on the back wall of the corrie is a long straight gully. Climb the gully. The first pitch is a vertical chimney, there are five pitches, alternating with easy slopes.

Spidean a'Choire Liath: South East Buttress.

—Pyramid Buttress. 600 ft. GRADE IV.

D. Jenkins, C. Rowland & M. Webster. February 1977.

This route climbs the skyline seen on the front cover of 'Northern Highlands' Vol. II. Following the initial slope, climb depression for 100 ft. until forced left into 20 ft. corner. Climb corner, go left to good stance. Climb up 10 ft. and move left to gain rib. Follow rib, one pitch, then go diagonally right into big couloir directly above the start. A 200 ft. slope leads to top.

Applecross: Sgùrr a'Chaorachain: North West Buttresses.

—No. 4 Gully. 500 ft. GRADE IV.

C. Rowland + A. C. Cain. February 1977.

The buttresses are split by five deep gullies; the following route climbs the fourth gully from the left. (This appears to be the gully between *Totem* and *Turret Buttresses*). After the initial ice pitch a huge cave is reached at 200 ft. Climb the steep pillar on right to easy slopes above (crux). Continue to where gully forks, take left fork leading to two short, awkward pitches and a final slope.

South East Wall.—*Big Daddy.*

R. Sharp & G. Shields. June 1972.   400 ft.   Hard Very Severe.

At the top of the mountain the plateau sports a radio mast; the following route lies on the cliff under this. At the left end of the face is a gully, start 100 ft. right of the gully, below an undercut groove. Climb through bottom overhang to undercut shallow corner. Using a peg to start, climb corner to gain small stance at top. Move hard right across overhung slab to gain a ledge, then go diagonally right across wall to narrow corner. Go up this, finishing in a wider corner to reach the plateau.

Beinn Bhan: Coire na Poite.—*Silver Tear.*

N. Muir & A. Paul. 12th February 1977.   1,000 ft.   GRADE V.

Right of *Mad Hatters Gully* is a prominent ice fall. Climb this for 850 ft Mixed climbing then leads to top. Occasional cornice.

Achnashellach: Fuar Tholl: South East Cliff.—*Ben Gunn.*

R. Sharp & G. Shields. June 1972.   500 ft.   Severe.

Start 100 ft. left of *Boat Tundra.* Climb short corners and ribs always moving rightwards to finish over large roof immediately above obvious black corner.

Mainreachan Buttress.—*Direct Route.*

R. Sharp & G. Shields. June 1972.   600 ft.   Severe.

Both this, and the next route are of a more direct nature than earlier lines. Start at right hand end of the nose at a recess, which continues as a groove. Take a direct line to below a steep, slabby wall, using grooves and corners. Climb crux wall via groove and rib, go rightwards at top and continue over short walls into a corner system behind a large detached flake.

—*All The Way.*

R. Sharp & G. Shields. June 1972.   500 ft.   Hard Very Severe.

Starts on shelf below *Investigator* and takes a direct line to obvious nose at top of cliff. (For relevant article on rock music, see *S.M.C.J.*, 1973, xxx, 143.) Go left on shelf to narrow corner. Climb steep wall then the corner to the gangway of *Investigator*, go left on this to below groove, gain this via a wall and roof, continue to recess, move right to below nose then left across bulge onto a slab. Finish as last pitch of *Investigator*.

Sgùrr Ruadh.—*Upper Buttress.*

First winter ascent.   900 ft.   GRADE III.

P. Nunn & A. Riley. February 1972.

This is the large, pear-shaped buttress right of *Raeburn's Buttress*, left of the big easy couloir. The lower section is somewhat steep and unconventional for the grade. The route taken was probably partly in common with *Original Route.* Climb corner at lower left side of buttress, escape right onto easier ground, then return back left up steep walls to gain a steep scoop. Climb the scoop, exit left, then climb steep ground directly to finish by an easier gully.

NORTHERN HIGHLANDS III

Loch Carron: Glas Bheinn: North Face.—*Black House.*
T. Briggs, P. Nunn & C. Rowland. April 1972. 590 ft. Very Severe.

Start below centre of crag. From a pinnacle go right up a crack (100 ft.). Go left round a rib and up a wide scoop (120 ft.). Climb directly, sometimes grassily, to a stance below overhangs and a small white slab (130 ft.). Climb slab on the left, traverse right, exit steeply on the right at a ledge and peg belay (80 ft.). This is the leftmost end of a long terrace. Finish directly up steep walls (160 ft.). Recommended.

—Adul Suh.
P. Braithwaite & P. Nunn. April 1974. 560 ft. Very Severe·

Start about 100 ft. left of *Black House*. Climb large groove, overhang and luminous green moss above. Escape right below overhang (120 ft.). Continue directly to below the steep grooves on the nose of the crag, just left of the white wall on *Black House* (220 ft.). Go left and finish by shallow chimneys (220 ft.).

Foinaven: Cnoc a'Mhadaidh: North Face.
There are now at least six routes on this cliff. (For *Quergang* see *S.M.C.J.*, 1973, xxx, 171; for *Pilastre*, *S.M.C.J.*, 1974, xxx, 270). The following four routes are described from left to right.

—East Slabs.
T. Lewis & R. Toogood. June 1975. 500 ft. Very Severe.

Climb the slabs at the east edge of the main crag, just right of the slit gully.

—Star Turn.
B. Griffiths, P. Nunn & R. Toogood. June 1976. 580 ft. Very Severe.

Start at large block left of *Pilastre*. Climb overlap a little to the left and up slab to ledge under roof (70 ft.). Go up crack left of roof and climb slabs to stance below black slab (120 ft.). Go up slab to overhanging wall, using a nut gain a hanging ramp and climb to small stance on upper slab (120 ft.). Climb up left then straight up, finishing up awkward wall at a flat shelf (130 ft.). Finish up groove and slabs, usually wet (140 ft.).

—The Great Roof.
P. Burke & R. S. Dearman. June 1975. 600 ft. Very Severe and A.3.

This route climbs the lower slabs right of *Quergang*, then follows the 60 ft. roof crack using large pegs. Above, finish by difficult free climbing.

—West Slabs.
R. S. Dearman & D. Moorhouse. June 1976. 600 ft. Very Severe and A.2/3.

Climb the lower slabs towards the right of the crag, then the great roof where a pillar abuts against it. The roof required about 7 pegs or other points of aid and was followed by several Very Severe pitches above.

Creag Urbhard.—*Whitewash.*   550 ft.   Very Severe.
B. Dunn & A. Paul. 11th August 1976.

This route lies between *Pantagruel* and *Gargantua*, trending rightwards to finish next to *Gargantua*. Start at easy angled slabs some 60 ft. left of the bottom corner of *Gargantua*. Peg belays used. Climb to right-hand end of prominent overhang, climb bulge using a crack which is followed to a belay (110 ft.). Above is a vague groove. Climb this directly for 70 ft. and traverse hard right to belay below large overhang (120 ft.). Climb right end of overhang using a rib, to reach foot of small blank wall. Turn the wall on its left by an overhanging groove then climb rightwards to belay at foot of prominent corner (100 ft.). Ascend corner to belay at point of steepening (90 ft.). Continue up corner to the 'rock gangway' (70 ft.). Above is the corner avoided by *Gargantua*, climb this to finish (60 ft.).

(See article and diagram this issue).

Lord Reay's Seat.—*Breakaway.*   500 ft.   Very Severe.
B. Dunn & A. Paul. 13th August 1976.

Start just left of *Pobble* (*S.M.C.J.*, 1973, xxx, 171). Climb 20 ft. to ledge at right of white rock scar, continue up leftward slanting groove to large flake belays on ledge (130 ft.). Climb wall above for 40 ft. to small ledge, continue up smooth groove, move rightwards to terrace (140 ft.). Climb groove immediately right of rock scar (120 ft.). Take easier rock to arête, belay below corner (150 ft.). Climb corner to top, as for *Pobble* (80 ft.). Peg belays used.

Cape Wrath: Creag Riabhach.

This crag lies some 4 miles N.W. of the Rhiconich-Durness road, and is best approached from a point half-a-mile N.E. of Gualin House. In the centre of the crag is a vertical and blank section of wall. 100 yards left of this is an overhanging and vegetated groove/crack line, climbed by the following very good, and hard route.

—*The Godfather.* 580 ft.   Hard Very Severe.
D. Marshall & C. Rowland. May 1972.

Start right of gully at vegetated, steep slab. Climb slab, trending rightwards, to belay in corner under steep left wall (130 ft.). Traverse right to groove and climb to top of pedestal (100 ft.). The first part of the corner above is blank. Climb short overganging chimney on left wall, exit onto blank slab (extremely difficult), move back right into corner and follow this to stance (130 ft.). Climb steep chimney crack on left (120 ft.). An easy gully leads to top (100 ft.).

The following route begins just left of *The Godfather*.

—*Masquerade.*   600 ft.   Hard Very Severe.
T. Howard & A. Maskery. June 1976.

About 150 ft. above the start is a terrace. This is reached by chimneys at the left side of the central scoop taken by *The Godfather* (150 ft.). Traverse left on the terrace and climb steep red cracks to stance below roof (140 ft.). Traverse left under roof and climb cracks, traverse right using one peg to gain cracks above initial line (120 ft.). Finish in two pitches (200 ft.).

—Herod's Evil. 630 ft. Hard Very Severe.
B. Griffiths, P. Nunn & R. Toogood. June 1976.

This route climbs the centre of the right-hand mass of the crag, following steep cracks and chimneys through overhanging walls. Start at recess chimney about 250 ft. right of the central scoop. Climb groove then right fork into steep crack, follow this to terraces with difficult landing and belay on high terrace (150 ft.). Climb right-hand groove (several pegs used to overcome vegetation, may be easier on later ascents), and a block-filled chimney to midway ledge (140 ft.). Continue up chimney to its closure, continue by steep crack to dangerous landing (peg runner), go up to higher belay on steep vegetation (130 ft.). Continue more reasonably in groove until short traverse left leads to ledge right of hanging slab (130 ft.). Climb steep corner right of slab then thin crack on left, loose blocks (80 ft.).

Kintail: Sgùrr na Carnach (Five Sisters).—*East Gully.*
C. Rowland. February 1976. 700 ft. GRADE II.

The gully is clearly seen approaching from the Allt a'Choire Domhain. It falls almost directly from the summit and may have been climbed before. One short pitch at mid-height.

CAIRNGORMS I

The Loch Avon Horseshoe: Shelter Stone Crag.—*Loki.*
A. Liddel & M. Burrows-Smith. June 1976. 400 ft. Very Severe.

This route climbs the slabs between *Thor* and *The Pin.* Climb slabs below the corner of *Thor* to gain the lower terrace (150 ft.). Move up and right on grass heading for corner right of *Thor.* Climb crack, then rib bounding corner, move left to old pegs in *Thor* corner, free climb *Thor* to hanging stance. Tension to foothold on right, climb corner for 12 ft. using aid (difficult), move right and using rope swing down onto stance of *The Pin.* (Presumably at top of second pitch—*Ed.*).

The following two routes lie on the unnamed crag west of *Pinnacle Gully.* (G.R. 998 015).

—Quartz Gully.
A. Fyffe + Miss E. Blair. Winter 1972. 300 ft. GRADE II/III.

This is the slabby gully at the far right of the cliff, bounded on its right by a well-defined rib. Climb the gully. The upper section may give a long but easy angled ice pitch.

—Garbh Gully.
A. Fyffe + Miss E. Blair. Winter 1972. 500 ft. GRADE III.

The obvious forked gully in the centre of the cliff. Climb the gully, taking the right fork.

Hell's Lum Crag.—*The Exorcist.*
A. Liddel & M. Burrows-Smith. Summer 1975. 340 ft. Very Severe.

Climb the leftward-facing corner between *Good Intentions* and *Hells Lump.* Start at the foot of *Hells Lump.* Climb easy chimney to grass break (75 ft.). Take wide crack above for 40 ft. then an ascending traverse right to corner. Climb corner, belay on right rib (115 ft.). Climb rib above to easy ground (150 ft.).

—The Omen.

A. Liddel & M. Burrows-Smith. July 1976.   550 ft.   Very Severe·

This route lies right of *Clean Sweep*. Start at base of easy ramp leading to *Deep Cut Chimney*. Gain slab above, follow lip of this in a left rising traverse (100 ft.). Go left then back right on ledge above, climb slab to below obvious left facing corner, belay on huge block (80 ft.). Climb the thin corner up left to belay on block of *Clean Sweep* (60 ft.). Climb crack 20 ft. right of *Clean Sweep* (100 ft.). Move up and right over bulge, then up pleasant quartz crack to good ledge (60 ft.). Climb wall above (150 ft.). Easy rock to finish.

—The Underworld.

B. Barton & A. Fyffe. 4th July 1976.   640 ft.   Very Severe.

Start about 20 ft. left of *The Wee Devil*; there is a green slab with thin crack at the foot of a diagonal fault. Climb crack and continuation corners (140 ft.). Go up left then over roof by obvious crack, go easily right to belay below corner, down and right of the main corner of *The Wee Devil* (120 ft.). Climb corner, just below final steepening move right onto rib. Go up slabs and walls (120 ft.). Move left into short pink corner, climb this and slab above to ledge, climb cracks above on edge overlooking *The Wee Devil* (140 ft.). Traverse left on hanging slab, gain fault on left of tower, climb fault to finish by obvious, overhanging niche (120 ft.).

The Stag Rocks: Longbow Crag.—*Addenda.*

A. Fyffe & W. March. 1972.   450 ft.   Very Severe.

Start right of *Sand-Pyper*, just left of vegetated depression. Climb up and slightly left for two pitches, crossing overlap at top of second pitch (common with *Sand-Pyper*), belay under large roof as for *Sand-Pyper*. Descend slightly and go round to left. Climb steep ramp and wall (crux). Continue up groove and crack with jutting block at top to reach easy ground.

Stac an Fharaidh: The West Face.—*Cherry.*

A. Liddel & M. Burrows-Smith. Summer 1975.   490 ft.   Very Severe.

Left of *Deluge* is an arrow-head-like formation with obvious corner on left. Start up left facing corner, climb slabs in two pitches to belay below obvious corner (200 ft.). Move left 20 ft., gain ledge above, traverse back right and make blind move onto slab above, belay on left (40 ft.). Climb slabs to the left (150 ft.). Finish up corner above (100 ft.).

The Northern Corries: Coire an Lochan: No. 4 Buttress.
—Transformer.   300 ft.   Very Severe.

B. Barton & A. Fyffe. June 1976.

This route girdles the central section of the buttress using the prominent horizontal fault. Start about 50 ft. left of *Savage Slit*, at a pink slab. Climb easily up and right to gain the groove above the obvious square roof. Follow the groove and its right wall and trend right to a peg belay in the groove of *Bulgy* (90 ft.). Descend 10 ft. and traverse into *Savage Slit* via the deep, horizontal crack (30 ft.). Go right on the obvious shelf and gain *Fallout Corner*. Descend its right edge a few feet to gain an exposed perch (60 ft.). Continue right under roofs, reverse *War and Peace* a few feet to jutting blocks, continue rightwards into *Procrastination* and climb that route to gain easy ground on the right (90 ft.). Finish easily rightwards or more directly upwards (30 ft.).

CAIRNGORMS II

Ben Macdhui: Coire Sputan Dearg.—*The Chebec.*   200 ft.   Very Severe.
G. Skelton & I. Vause. 28th June 1975.

This route takes a line on the left of *Spider Buttress*, at a cigar-shaped overhang. Start directly below this by scrambling up to the foot of a corner, belay (30 ft.). Move left and climb grooves to right end of the overhang, move right (crux), climb cracks to ledge and belay (120 ft.). Go left and climb rightward overhung corner to horizontal crack, traverse right then up more easily to finish (50 ft.).

—The Hin'most.
R. Archbold & G. S. Strange. 20th June 1976.   250 ft.   Very Severe.

On the slab-wall right of *Terminal Wall*. Climb first pitch of *Terminal Wall* to belay ledge. Make a long rightwards rising traverse following obvious parallel folds. Where the folds almost meet the flanking gully go up left to foot of prominent crack in centre of wall. Climb just right of crack then step left and finish directly up crack.

Creagan a'Choire Etchachan: The Crimson Slabs.—*Dagger.*
A. Nisbet & A. Robertson. 29th January 1977.   500 ft.   GRADE IV·

The original summer line was followed throughout. The dièdre was straightforward on snow ice, but in leaner conditions could be very hard. In good conditions the final pitch will be the crux, particularly if plastered. Escape is possible down the gangway below this pitch, the route would then probably be a III/IV.

Beinn a'Bhuird: Coire na Ciche.—*High Step.*   550 ft.   Hard Very Severe.
J. Moreland & D. Wright. September 1976.

A companion route to *Three Step*, taking a rightward trending line above that route. Start right of *The Carpet*. Cross a large diagonal slab, belay below first wall (110 ft.). Climb break in wall, trending leftwards till stopped by loose blocks. Gain second slab and cross this to belay below second wall (80 ft.). Climb corner crack and traverse grass ramp (150 ft.). Finish as for *Three Step* (two pitches).

—Hell's Bells.   620 ft.   Very Severe.
S. Falconer, G. Reilly, I. Reilly & G. Stephen. 18th July 1976.

Follows a line midway between *Vatican Steps* and *Quartzvein Route.* Start at foot of *Quartzvein* and climb directly to a prominent short leaning corner, midway between the huge block on *Vatican Steps* and the buttress edge (200 ft.). Climb corner then slabs to grassy ledge below overlap (80 ft.). Climb overlap, go up then left to a triangular niche at overlap. Climb this to poor belay (80 ft.). Climb bulge, go left then up to obvious overlap break, climb break and trend rightwards to large grass ledge (140 ft.). Traverse left then up ramp rightwards to plateau (120 ft.). A good route on clean rock throughout, but poorly protected.

CAIRNGORMS V

Eagle's Rock.—*Indolence.*   400 ft.   GRADE III.
A. Nisbet & A. Robertson. 12th December 1976.

Early in the season, a prominent icefall usually forms on the summer line. Climb the icefall into the obvious gully above, finish up the gully. A fine climb, better and harder than *Lethargy*.

—Nomad's Crack.   300 ft.   GRADE IV.
A. Nisbet & A. Robertson. 26th December 1976.

A good, sustained climb on a narrow ribbon of ice throughout. From the vee chimney climb straight up to the final groove. The last 20 ft. were devoid of ice and gave strenuous rock moves.

—Abstention.   350 ft.   GRADE IV.
A. Nisbet & A. Robertson. 28th December 1976.

Short, but sustained and varied. Climb a gully on the right to 50 ft. beyond the summer start, trend left to gain shallow ice gully. Climb to below nose and traverse well right to reach parallel ice gully leading to top.

—Gibber.   450 ft.   GRADE III/IV.
A. Nisbet & N. Spinks. 2nd February 1977.

A sliver of ice follows approximately the summer line; but a good build-up is necessary. The 'roofed corner' was seriously unprotected on thin ice.

—Whisper.   450 ft.   GRADE III/IV.
A. Nisbet & A. Robertson. 20th February 1977.

A parallel line of ice forms on the slab right of *Gibber*. Start at the lowest rocks and climb the ice over several bulges.

Creag an Dubh Loch: South East Buttress.—*Leftovers.*
A. Nisbet & A. Robertson. 19th February 1977.   400 ft.   GRADE II.

This is the obvious, discontinuous snow ramp, starting well left and slanting up and right to the top.

—Hanging Garden Route,
Left Fork.   400 ft.   GRADE IV.
A. Nisbet & A. Robertson. 6th January 1977.

Follow the original winter ascent but continue straight up the groove above until a steep wall forces a leftward traverse across an exposed slab to gain easy ground. No cornice difficulties on this ascent but there often will be and a further traverse left may be necessary. This route may often be the easiest route out of *The Hanging Garden*.

Glen Clova: Red Craigs: The Doonie.—*Cream Cracker.*
                                    200 ft.   Hard Very Severe, A.2.
D. Myatt & C. Robinson. 13th November 1976.

This route lies on the steep wall right of *Larch Tree Wall*. It is at least partly in common with a route known as *Trapeze*, climbed in the early '60's, but is recorded here for posterity. On the right of the wall is an obvious slab; start on the right edge of this. Climb short wall to ledge below overhang, traverse left then up to obvious fault in roof of overhang (crux). Climb this using 2 or 3 nuts and continue up steep slab on right to wall. Traverse left on steep, loose rock to crack, above this move right to tree belays (120 ft.). Climb flake moving left then up to overhung wall. Traverse left to corner, tree above, climb corner and finish up crack system on wall above (80 ft.).

CENTRAL HIGHLANDS

Creag Meaghaidh:—*Raeburn's Gully Buttress.* 1,500 ft. GRADE III.
P. C. Webster & A. L. Wielochowski. 30th December 1976.

This climbs the buttress edge immediately left of *Raeburn's Gully.* The upper section is frequently taken to avoid deep snow in the gully. Start at the right of the buttress. Follow easy grooves to a horizontal ledge; this is just below the level of the true beginning of the gully. Traverse left along the ledge for 200 ft. to reach a large block. Go back right for 80 ft. to gain the crest of the buttress. Climb the crest, trending left where possible. The remaining 1,000 ft. can be climbed anywhere at an easier standard.

Pinnacle Buttress.—*Vanishing Ledge.*
1,200 ft. GRADE IV/V·
J. P. Nash & A. L. Wielochowski. 22nd February 1976.

This is a girdle traverse of *Pinnacle Buttress,* starting at the foot of *Smith's Gully* and finishing on easy ground left of *Easy Gully.* The main section of this traverse has been known as *Vanishing Ledge* since at least 1937; it lies parallel to, and some 300 ft. below *Apollyon Ledge.* Start as for *Smith's Gully.* Climb *Smith's Gully* for 50 ft., traverse right along ledges, peg runners, to reach a small stance (110 ft., crux). Follow the ledge which becomes progressively easier to reach *Easy Gully.*
(See Central Highlands Notes).

Creag an Lochain (about one mile north of Creag
Meaghaidh summit).—*Fox Trot.* 250 ft. GRADE IV
D. K. R. Nottidge & A. L. Wielochowski. 13th March 1976.

Some 300 ft. short of the left edge of the main cliffs of Creag an Lochain is an ice fall. This is composed of three sections which may merge into one great sheet. This route climbs the central fall direct. Climb the introductory gully below the ice fall, to gain a ledge and peg belays. Climb the ice fall.

Chno Dearg: Meall Garbh: East Face.

This cliff lies about 10 miles south-west of Loch Laggan. (O.S. 1″ Sheet No. 47, G.R. 373 727). It may be reached in 50 minutes from a forestry track, most of the way by a good path. (See *S.M.C.J.*, 1968, xxix, 69, where P. Tranter describes two summer routes). The cliff provides several short winter routes of various grades, and may be a useful alternative when the higher climbing areas are out of condition.

The main buttress is split by a deep gash, a central gully, which contains a giant chockstone near the top. It is as yet unclimbed. On the right the buttress is bounded by a broad gully, the entrance of which is barred by an ice pitch. The left side of the main buttress is defined by a deep chimney line, left of which are steep walls. On the extreme left is the small, *Terminal Buttress.* Several easy lines have been climbed left of the steep walls. The following routes are described.

—*The Ramp.*
A. L. Wielochowski. 3rd February 1976. 600 ft. GRADE II/III.

This is the obvious left trending ramp cutting across the steep walls left of the main buttress. Access to the ramp is by a steep angled rightwards traverse from the foot of the walls.

—The Frozen Vice.

G. Thomas & A. L. Wielochowski. 20th March 1976.   350 ft.   GRADE IV.

This route climbs the deep chimney line just right of the steep walls. Climb the steep, wide chimney (crux). Continue in the line of the original chimney to finish up a very narrow slit, containing a short, steep ice pitch at half height.

The next three routes lie close together, at the right end of the main buttress. They probably offer the best climbing on the cliff and are described from right to left.

—Broad Gully. 500 ft.   GRADE III.

J. Crowden & A. L. Wielochowski. 1st April 1976.

This is the straight, broad gully right of the main buttress. Climb the introductory steep ice pitch. Above, another short ice pitch leads to the easy upper section.

—Ping Pong.   500 ft.   GRADE II.

A. L. Wielochowski. 30th March 1976.

From the foot of the *Broad Gully* ice pitch, climb a shallow, left-trending gully for 100 ft., then move back right into *Broad Gully.* Follow it for 80 ft. then take an ice gully off to the left. Various finishes possible.

—Deep Slit Gully.

A. L. Wielochowski. 4th February 1976.   450 ft.   GRADE II/III.

Start in a very deep, narrow gully, about 80 ft. left of the start of *Broad Gully.* After 150 ft. trend slightly leftwards.

Newtonmore: Creag Dubh: Central Wall.—*Men Only.*

220 ft.   Hard Very Severe.

D. Cuthbertson & A. Taylor. 23rd September 1976.

On the gully wall left of *King Bee.* Steep and sustained. To start, either climb the first pitch of *Run Free* (see below), and traverse left, or scramble for about 100 ft. to gain a ledge left of a green wall. Traverse right to a groove on the green wall, climb the groove and its roof direct to tree ledge, continue up wall, climb second roof, good chockstone, then make left traverse to stance and flake belay (130 ft.). Climb wall to roof, turn this on right and continue to junction with *King Bee.* Where *King Bee* goes right continue to another roof, climb this and wall above to finish.

—Run Free.

D. Cuthbertson & D. Jamieson. 23rd July 1976.   300 ft.   Hard Very Severe.

A good route ranking with the best at Creag Dubh. Start at open corner just left of *King Bee.* Climb corner until a traverse left leads to stance and small tree (80 ft.). Go back right to tree, climb short grey wall to break in roof, climb this and continue to stance on *King Bee* (70 ft.). Traverse right and follow crack in rib above until short left traverse leads to black groove capped by small roof. Climb groove and traverse back onto steep rib to finish as for *The Organ Grinder* (150 ft.).

—Inbred—Direct Finish.

R. Anderson & D. Cuthbertson. September 1976.   100 ft.   Hard Very Severe.

This takes the obvious line of weakness from the *Inbred* niche to the last part of *Strapadicktaemi* (see below). Climb *Inbred* to belay in the niche. Climb thin crack directly above niche to reach the ramp on the normal route, continue directly above over two bulges to gain the final crack of *Strapadicktaemi.* Finish up the crack.

—Strapadicktaemi.
210 ft.   Hard Very Severe.

R. Anderson & D. Cuthbertson. 25th September 1976.

Take a line between *Inbred* and *The Minge*, following an obvious diagonal crack left of the slabs of *Migraine* in its upper part. Climb *Inbred* for a few feet then take an obvious hand traverse crack out right to junction with *The Minge*. Where that route goes right, continue up to and over bulge, moving leftwards to stance on *Inbred* (90 ft.). Traverse right, climb left slanting crack until traverse left leads to block beneath another crack. Climb crack to finish (120 ft.).

—Ticket To Ride.
120 ft.   Hard Very Severe.

D. Cuthbertson & A. Taylor. 23rd September 1976.

A fine pitch, better than its companion routes *Sweetness* and *The Mighty Piston*. Start just right of *The Mighty Piston*, and just left of an obvious black streak. Traverse up and right to a good flake, climb direct to obvious niche at two thirds height. From niche move out left and climb steep wall to finish (120 ft.).

—The Frustrations.

D. Cuthbertson & A. Taylor. October 1976.   230 ft.   Hard Very Severe.

This is a left to right girdle of the lower wall from *Rib Direct* to *Fred*. Start from the rightmost ledge right of the first pitch of *Rib Direct*. Climb *Rib Direct*, traverse right along to the end of the ledges (80 ft.). From the ledge make an awkward move down a few feet, make some delicate moves across quartz bands, continue in same line to belay in chimney of *Cunnulinctus* (70 ft.). Descend a few feet, traverse right then down to belay on *Phellatio*, traverse right to block on *Tongue Twister*, reverse that route to top of ivy then traverse right to finish up *Mirador* (80 ft.).

Binnein Shuas: Eastern Sector.—*Hurricane.*   480 ft.   Very Severe.
C. Ogilvie & Miss C. Stock. 11th September 1976.

This route starts on the wall right of Hidden Gully, between *Flypaper* and *Hairline Grooves*, and crosses *Uisge-Beatha* at mid height. Start in *Hidden Gully*, about 20 ft. below first step; a tree is visible on wall above. Climb shallow corner past rock scar, continue in faint groove to tree, move up left to belay on another tree (130 ft.). From tree gain rib on right, follow this easily to belay (80 ft.). Go down right onto fine slab, climb this centrally, take overhang directly then slab above, trending rightwards to small flake belay on terrace (170 ft.). Climb slab above (100 ft.).

—Whipped Cream.   260 ft.   Hard Severe.

D. Baker & M. Smith. 15th August 1976.

Start just left of flat block, left of *Soft Shoe Shuffle*. Climb left trending fault to blaeberry ledge, follow corner crack above to small ledge on right, nut belays high on right (130 ft). From right end of ledge go up and right across white slab to below small bay. Gain bay, climb overhangs above, turn second set of overhangs on left to ledge and nut belays. An enjoyable pitch (130 ft.). 300 ft. of scrambling leads to terrace.

BEN NEVIS

North East Buttress: Minus One Buttress.—*Minus One Direct*
—*The Serendipity Line.*   Very Severe.
K. V. Crocket & I. Fulton. 27th August 1972.

This should be regarded as the true direct line of the buttress, rather than the original direct line, which veers off to give several poor pitches in *Minus One Gully*, and a later variation (see *S.M.C.J.*, 1970, xxix, 312), which avoids the crux. The present variation was climbed accidentally, without guidebook, and only a later ascent following the original line gave a belated recognition of what is surely one of the best routes on the hill. It must have been climbed by other parties in similar circumstances.

Climb the original line through the crux to below the wide crack. Go left to the crest of the buttress and follow this to the overhangs. Find a line through the overhangs leading to the great flake and finish by the original line.

                              —*Minus One Buttress.*   850 ft.   GRADE V.
N. Muir & A. Paul. 5th April 1977.

Climb *North Eastern Grooves* to overhang at 300 ft. Break out right and up to join *Minus One Direct*. Follow this to beyond left traverse on loose wall, climb *Minus One Direct* to shattered arête, finishing on North East Buttress.

                       Douglas Boulder.—*South West Ridge.*
G. Mackenzie & C. Stead. 14th November 1976.   500 ft.   GRADE III.
Summer route followed.

GLENCOE, GLEN ETIVE & ARDGOUR

Buachaille Etive Mór: Creag a'Bhancair.—*Le Monde.*
N. Colton & W. Todd. 4th June 1976.   160 ft.   Hard Very Severe.

Start 70 ft. right of *Carnivore* at a groove beside a small pinnacle. Climb groove until it fades, traverse right to shallow scoop, climb scoop and bulge, step left then go straight up to the pegs on *Carnivore* pitch one (80 ft.). Follow the leftward slanting fault to the top (80 ft.).

                              —*Reptile.*   240 ft.   Severe.
C. Heep & G. Skelton. May 1975.

Start from top of large pedestal at right end of crag. Climb crack and chimney to belay on ledge (120 ft.). Continue to top (120 ft.).

Bidean nam Bian: Aonach Dubh: Lower North East Nose.—*Venison Dagger.*   250 ft.   Very Severe.
A. Paul, G. Reilly & J. Reilly. 30th October 1976.

Start 10 ft. right of *Original Route*. Climb small chimney crack then a rib leftwards to foot of obvious open corner and ledge (100 ft.). Climb corner, exiting rightwards at top to belay (70 ft.). Continue in same line over short walls to top (80 ft.).

West Face: E. Buttress.

—The Fly Man. 230 ft. Hard Very Severe.

N. Colton & W. Todd. 23rd June 1976.

Takes arête right of *Hee Haw*. Start in gully right of that climb; a fault splits the gully wall. Climb fault to belay at top of *Hee Haw* pitch one (50 ft.). Swing onto the rib and climb to obvious flake, climb this and continue past two small ledges until it is possible to move rightwards round the arête to small ledge below thin crack. Climb crack to flake belay (130 ft.). Climb wall above to top (50 ft.).

Stob Coire nam Beith.—*Cleftweave.* 1,300 ft. GRADE II/III.

B. Clarke & A. Strachan. January 1972.

Well to the right of *North West Gully*, follow a series of gullies which wind up immediately left of *The Pyramid*, and so reach a snowfield overlooking *Summit Gully*. A steep, short ice wall on the left leads to another gully system. Follow this to a small amphitheatre, move up into a short gully on the right and climb an ice pitch to exit onto the summit slopes.

Garbh Bheinn of Ardgour: Subsidiary Buttresses: Garbh Choire Buttress.—*Cantata.* 300 ft. Very Severe.

K. V. Crocket & I. Fulton. 24th July 1976.

This is the central line on the buttress. (See *S.M.C.J.*, 1976, xxxi, 58). Scramble to where a downward jutting nose abuts on a slab, begin at loose flake. Climb up and slightly right, go left then up corner to stance (60 ft.). Climb corner above, peg runner (60 ft.). Climb wall on left to slab, follow this to belay below twin steep grooves (50 ft.). Go right and up to good flake crack, traverse left across wall to gain slab above twin grooves. Follow slab to easy ground (130 ft.). The twin grooves would give a harder, more direct finish.

South Wall of Great Ridge: Bottom Tier.

—Mournblade. 200 ft. Very Severe.

K. V. Crocket, C. D. Grant & J. A. P. Hutchinson. 31st July 1976.

The main feature of this route is a corner, some 40 ft. right of and parallel to the *Butterknife* corner. Start 20 ft. right of *Butterknife* at a rough flake. Climb up, then right to the foot of the corner. Follow the corner, step right into a groove and so to good stance at a pinnacle. Climb bulge directly above on good holds and continue more easily.

Glen Creran: Beinn Sgulaird: South West Face: The Sgulaird Slabs.

These were explored by G. N. Hunter and N. Quinn and the routes described were all made between 29th August and 5th September 1976.

The main slabs are about 600 ft. high and are composed of solid, clean granite. In the centre are large overlaps with good cracks for nuts. Above the main slab is the *Upper Slab*, while over on the right is the *Bealach Crag*, and on its right, below, the *Lower Bealach Slabs*. The best and longest climbs are on the *Main Slab*, and are described from left to right. Peg belays are required on most routes.

—Safari. 640 ft. Hard Severe.

Start at arrow on lowest rock on left of slab. Climb slab direct then trend left to belay (150 ft.). Follow large slab corner, move left to belay on small ledge (130 ft.). Climb left then right above large semi-detached blocks to belay on right (90 ft.). Continue directly up smooth slab above, move left then up and through overlaps, follow slab above to second overlap, break through and follow good cracks to belay (150 ft.). Move up leftwards into corner then up through overlap to finish up crest of ridge (120 ft.).

—*Majuba.*   530 ft.   Severe.
Start at arrow on lowest rocks. Climb slab direct (150 ft.). Continue
directly up slab right of corner then trend right small overlap, break through
overlap on right, climb left then directly to belay (140 ft.). Climb corner above
direct to large overlaps, break through crack and grooves to belay on small
stance (90 ft.). Continue directly via grooves and small overlap to terminal
overlap, climb this directly to finish (150 ft.).

—*Tokalosh.*   550 ft.   Very Severe.
Start right of *Majuba.* Climb easy rounded slab to belay (150 ft.). Trend
right to bow-shaped corner on central slab, climb to top of corner, step right
onto thin slab, up then trend left to shallow scoop, up to belay (150 ft.).
Climb steep grooves above thin slab to belay below large overlaps (100 ft.).
Climb up to corner, large blocks, climb overhang into grooves, follow these
directly to rock nose then small corner slab. Belay under blocks at grass
ledge (150 ft.).

—*Assegai.*   520 ft.   Very Severe.
Start at arrow on right side of slab. Climb easy corner on slab to grass
patch, climb overlap above to belay (150 ft.). Climb grooves above (140 ft.).
Continue up steep slab and grooves (140 ft.). Finish up corner groove
above (90 ft.).

Upper Slabs.
The following two routes climb the two obvious curving faults through
overlaps in a series of steps.

—*39 Steps.*   300 ft.   Severe.
This is the left fault. Start at arrow, follow small corners trending left to
belay (170 ft.). Follow cracks and grooves right, climb up and through overlaps (130 ft.).

—*Tiptoe.*   300 ft.   Severe.
Start at arrow. Climb obvious fault line right of 39 *Steps* in the centre
of the slab. Break through overlaps on good holds.

Bealach Crag.—*Creran Corner.*   235 ft.   Severe.
This route lies on the small but very good and steep granite slab below
the Bealach Coire Allt Buidhe. Climb directly up into obvious large corner,
follow this to belay on ledge (130 ft.). Climb slab to overlap, trend right to
second overlap then slab above to belay on ledge (80 ft.). Climb wall above
belay to finish.

SOUTHERN HIGHLANDS

Beinn an Dothaidh: North East Coire.
There has been some confusion regarding the position of *Haar* in this
coire. The accompanying diagram should dispel any mist. We can only add
that we consider this recently-developed area to give better climbing than
say, Stob Coire nan Lochan, Glencoe (though not as aesthetic). We
recommend any of the routes at GRADE III and above. The following routes
are described from left to right.

North West Buttress.—*The Skraeling.*
I. Fulton & J. Hutchinson. February 1976.   800 ft.   GRADE IV.
This route climbs the buttress immediately left of *Haar* and follows the
obvious steep corner line. Climb the easier angled lower tier to reach the
broad terrace below the main buttress. This point may be reached by
traversing in from the right. Left of the corner are slabs. These were
climbed followed by a difficult right traverse to gain the foot of the corner.
The corner was climbed in two steep pitches followed by easier grooves.

West Buttress.

As a separate entity, *Twofold Gully* does not exist; it was in fact an ascent of *Haar*. (For *Haar*, see *S.M.C.J.*, 1973, xxx, 182). The following route climbs a line just right of *Haar*.

—*Stormbringer*. 500 ft. GRADE III.

K. V. Crocket & I. Fulton. 3rd January 1977.

Start at foot of *Haar*. Gain ledge on right, step up, make rising right traverse to belay in corner. Continue directly by shallow gully and varied climbing.

—*Slow March*. 650 ft. GRADE IV.

C. D. Grant & C. Stead. 28th December 1976.

Start at the right edge of West Buttress, some 20 ft. left of *Cirrus* (see below). Climb up and left to a snow bay (belay). Go up and right to overhanging corner, follow ramp leftward to wide triangular corner (belay). Step down and traverse horizontally left 50 ft. to an ice groove, follow groove for 100 ft. when an easy traverse left leads to pleasant snow and ice grooves and so to top.

—*Cirrus*. 450 ft. GRADE III/IV.

J. Crawford, J. Gillespie & W. Skidmore. 24th March 1974.

This is the right bounding line of West Buttress. The route is a gully line, very narrow in its lower reaches. Climb the gully. The main pitch was 30 ft. of steep ice at about mid height. There may be at least two other ice pitches.

—*Far West Buttress*.

C. D. Grant & C. Stead. 3rd January 1977. 450 ft. GRADE III.

This is the buttress right of West Buttress, separated from it by *Cirrus*. Start at the left edge. Go up and right by a ramp to a chimney, climb this to belay. Go left a few feet and back right by a ramp to a ledge. Go right 50 ft. to a groove which leads to the top.

—*Clonus*. 400 ft. GRADE III/IV.

D. Hodgson & W. Skidmore. 26th December 1976.

This is the rightward facing corner about 80 ft. right of *Cirrus*. Climb the corner and iced slabs to good stance and belay above small slot (120 ft.). Climb slabs to overhanging barrier pitch in corner, peg runner in place, climb groove right of corner for 15 ft., difficult, gain ledge and traverse left across top of corner to easy snow. A rising right traverse leads back into corner and belay (140 ft.). Continue up corner, now almost a gully, to top (140 ft.). Escape is possible under the crux by taking snow shelf to right.

Ben Dorain: Coire an Dothaidh.—*Scorpion*. 350 ft. Very Severe.

R. Richardson & A. Walker. 21st August 1976.

This route lies on the crag on the north flank of Ben Dorain, further right than Creag Coire an Dothaidh (*S.M.C.J.*, 1976, xxxi, 59). The excellence of the rock belies its appearance. In the centre of the face are waterworn slabs. Start at short conspicuous rib on left. Climb rib to good stance and poor belays. Climb steep slab on right for 75 ft., awkward finish onto grass ledge (no protection). Follow ledge left to foot of corner crack. Climb crack, awkward left exit, traverse right a few feet then climb easy slabs to top.

Glen Orchy: Beinn Udlaidh: Coire Daimh.—*The Cramp.*

I. F. Duckworth & G. Skelton. 16th January 1977.   400 ft.   GRADE IV.

Left of *Quartzvein Scoop* is a large icefall. This route lies between *Quartzvein Scoop* and the icefall. Start to left of lowest rocks. Climb the first 120 ft. of the icefall to belay up on right. Traverse right 50 ft. to edge overlooking *Quartzvein Scoop,* climb short wall to belay. Climb to vertical rock wall, using peg for aid reach a ledge and go leftward to belay on pedestal. Follow obvious ice chute and continue rightwards to cornice finish.

—Ramshead Gully.

G. H. Caplan & I. D. Crofton. 4th December 1976.   300 ft.   GRADE III.

Easy climbing leads to a narrow chimney with an overhanging chockstone (crux). The gully then widens. Finish up a steep pitch, exiting right onto slabs.

The Cobbler: South Peak.—*North Wall Groove.*   350 ft.   GRADE IV.

N. Muir & A. Paul. 16th February 1977.

Climb *Sesame Groove* and continue up *North Wall Groove* to top.

Creag Tharsuinn.—*Trilogy.*   200 ft.   Very Severe.

D. Hodgson & W. Skidmore. 8th August 1976.

On the vertical buttress wall immediately left of *McLaren's Chimney.* Start centrally beneath undercut bulge crossing face. Climb wall to bulge, traverse right and climb bulge using high holds (sling useful) to gain juniper ledge. Climb crack on left to enter black groove on right leading to overhung recess. Exit left and move right to grass ledge and belays; sustained (100 ft.). Return left and climb wall on good holds, belay on right (50 ft.). Go down and left to prominent crack, follow crack to top (50 ft.).

Ben Ime.—*Hanging Groove.*   550 ft.   GRADE III/IV.

C. D. Grant & C. Stead. 26th December 1976.

Start as for the *Left Hand Start* to *Ben's Fault.* Climb corner (150 ft.). Climb hanging groove on left bounding rib to gain crest of rib (150 ft.). The rib then leads directly to the top via some awkward walls.

—Buttress Route.   500 ft.   GRADE III.

D. Jenkins, A. Pettit & C. Stead. 5th December 1976.

Start 30 ft. right of *Ben's Fault.* Climb up and right, finishing by a chimney.

—Forked Gully.   500 ft.   GRADE II.

J. Mackenzie. November 1976 (Right Fork).

C. D. Grant & C. Stead. 26th December 1976 (Left Fork).

This narrow gully bounds *Fan Gully Buttress* on the right, before the easy slopes of *Fan Gully.* A 60 ft. ice pitch leads to snow and further on the gully forks.

The Brack.—*Lilliput.*   170 ft.   Very Severe.

G. Skelton & A. Wilson. 19th September 1976.

On the left of the coire is the 'conspicuous pinnacle,' mentioned in the guide book. To right of pinnacle are two obvious cracks. This route starts round to the right on steep, slabby face. The face is right of a fault line and below a small overhang. Climb to overhang, go diagonally left to fault, continue up and left then move up to small ledge. Traverse right to grass ramp, climb this to belay and poor stance (110 ft.). Climb groove above, move right to grass ledge then finish up right hand arete.

—Right Hand Route.   300 ft.   GRADE IV.

N. Muir & A. Paul. 24th February 1977.

Climb *Great Central Groove* to gain very obvious ice ramp on right.
Climb ramp to top.

Beinn an Lochain: North East Coire.—*Monolith Grooves.*

B. Clarke & J. Mackenzie. 16th January 1977.   520 ft.   GRADE IV.

In the centre of the coire is a huge plinth of rock split by a prominent
corner and topped by two overhanging masses of rock. This is left of
Raeburn's Route. The following complex route climbs hidden lines of
weakness to and up the corner, and is very steep and fine. Start 100 ft. left of
the plinth. Climb shelves to a rock wall, traverse right to peg belay (100 ft.).
Go right and down into deep narrow gully, climb this to cave and flake belays.
In lean conditions, combined tactics may be necessary to gain the cave
(140 ft.). Go right from cave to exposed arête and climb steep rocks to belay
on huge ledge—'The Table' (30 ft.). Traverse down and left then across a
steep hanging ramp to belay at foot of left slanting chimney (100 ft.). Climb
chimney past bulging exit and follow steep snow to flake belay in huge roofed
cave—'The Gallery' (50 ft.). Above is the impressive and very steep final
corner. Climb this, passing overhang at 20 ft. (thread runner), continue more
easily to finish on steep snow. Short persons may need a sling at the overhang (100 ft.).

                                             —do.   Very Difficult.

J. Mackenzie. 3rd September 1976.

In summer follow the same line as in winter, but enter the gully more
directly, and instead of descending to the traverse from The Table, go up short
grooves then down left through a tunnel to gain the chimney.

—Promenade Gully.

M. Asturz & J. Mackenzie. 6th February 1977.   500 ft.   GRADE II.

Start 100 ft. left of the plinth, as for *Monolith Grooves.* Climb directly
up past a narrowing in the gully to below a steep cave (prominent pinnacle
high on left). Go left and round a wall to climb shelf parallel with main gully.
Climb past narrowing then right to rejoin main gully. Continue to fan-shaped
exit, heavily corniced on this ascent. Pleasant and interesting.

Loch an Restil Face.—*Twin Caves Gully.*

A. Craig & J. Mackenzie. 5th December 1976.   300 ft.   GRADE II/III.

This narrow gully lies at the north end of the face above the lochan.
Snow and ice lead to a through route then into a cave. The right wall gave a
steep ice pitch. A second cave can be passed on the right to finish.

Dunkeld: Craig-y-Barns: Lower Cave Crag.—*Paramour's Rib.*

B. Clarke & G. Rooney. 31st October 1976.   80 ft.   Very Severe.

To the right of *Cherry Tree Rib* is a prominent, right-angled corner;
immediately right of this is a fine arête. Climb the arête directly.

Upper Cave Crag.—*Tumbleweed.*

D. Cuthbertson & D. Jamieson. June 1976.   110 ft.   Hard Very Severe.

This takes the ramp and hanging corner well left of *The Gnome.* Climb
Flook a few feet then make a rightwards traverse to belay below holly bush
(30 ft.). Climb obvious ramp on left to reach a ledge. Move right and climb
shallow groove finishing up steep wall (80 ft.).

—*Death's Head.*   100 ft.   Hard Very Severe.
D. Cuthbertson, M. Hamilton & A. Taylor. October 1976.

Climb the steep cracked groove right of *Coffin Arête*. Climb easy rocks to belay as for *Coffin Arête* (20 ft.). Climb groove, avoiding initial groove on right.

Polney Crag.—*The Beginning.*   120 ft.   Hard Very Severe.
D. Cuthbertson & D. Jamieson. June 1976.

Climb first pitch of *Terminal Buttress* to thread belay. Climb steep groove down and right of the belay and take a line parallel to that route to the top.

(See Southern Highlands Notes).

Dumbarton Rock.—*Fever Pitch.*   90 ft.   Hard Very Severe.
N. Colton & W. Todd. 3rd June 1976.

Climb the arête left of *Longbow*. Start just right of the arête. Climb straight up until a move left brings a resting place at half height. Finish up the arête.

—*Gaucho.*   90 ft.   Hard Very Severe.
N. Donnelly & W. Todd. 24th August 1976.

Climb the arête left of *Desperado*. Climb the true start to *Desperado*, cross slab to the arête, finish up the arête (peg runner).

REGIONAL NOTES

Skye

Sgùrr na Stri.—Wilderness area. We have note of a short route on this peaklet. This would seem a good time to declare the climbing here pleasant, scenic, and reserved as an area best left for future unspoilt exploratory scrambling. We can mention in the passing that the buttresses lie above the Elgol-Coruisk path.

Arran

Coire nam Ceum.—*Entasis—Direct Variation.* C. Macadam, Summer 1975. Instead of traversing right to the first stance of *Fuoco*, from the finish of the chimney on the first pitch climb straight up over two ledges to 15 ft. below the top chimney; go left to a flake edge which is climbed to the ledge below the chimney.

Northern Highlands

Foinaven.—*Dionard Buttress No. 5?* We have note of a route which 'probably' lies on the same buttress as *Smick* (*S.M.C.J.*, 1975, xxx, 385). The initial responsibility for accurate reporting lies with the party of the first ascent, who by referring to earlier descriptions can relate their doings (usually), to other routes. Photographs and sketches are often useful and always accepted. However we will file such routes until they can be rationalised.

Cairngorms

Lochnagar and Creag an Dubh Loch. The summer of '76 was one of the driest on record, and consequently the big cliffs saw a fair level of activity. Details of recent first ascents in these areas will appear in the forthcoming S.M.T. Guide, expected this year, but as an appetiser the following notes may be of interest.

Creag an Dubh Loch. There were five new routes, including two impressive lines on the Broad Terrace Wall between *Culloden* and *Falkenhorst* (Dinwoodie). Most of the major routes had at least one ascent, and we can now confirm the following levels of aid—*Last Oasis* (no aid), *Sword of Damocles* (no aid, bolts avoided on left), *The Giant* (two points of aid on lower pitches), *Cougar* (seven points of aid), *Vampire* (three points of aid), and *Falseface* (four points of aid on leaning corner).

Lochnagar. There were six new routes, four of which were on the Black Spout Pinnacle. Perhaps one of the more outstanding new climbs of the season was Dinwoodie and Smith's *Blackspout Wall*. This is a direct ascent of the Pinnacle, starting in the Spout and taking the imposing wall right of *The Link*. As a prelude the previous day, the same team made the second ascent of *Mort*, with no aid. They report that the climbing on *Mort* is excellent, and that like Forbes and Rennies other Tough-Brown Face route, *Crypt*, it deserves to become a modern classic.

—*Grovel Wall*. 500 ft. GRADE IV. M. Freeman & A. Nisbet. 5th February 1977. This route has had earlier, incomplete ascents; the top half by Strange and party (1968), the lower part by Cohen (1975). Both these parties used the escape into *Pinnacle Gully One* at mid height. On this complete ascent the route name was most appropriate, most of the features being obscured by deep powder. A direct line was taken from The Mound to the Pinnacle summit. From the left edge of The Mound, climb diagonally rightwards to below the 'hanging block' (70 ft.). Cut back left and climb straight up to a short overhanging wall (120 ft.). Avoid this on the right and climb a direct line of grooves and shallow chimneys parallel with *Pinnacle Gully One* to the top of The Pinnacle.

Glen Clova: The Doonie: North West Face. We note the following routes free from aid—*The Witches Tooth* (Very Severe), *Zig Zag Direct* (Very Severe) and *Red Wall* (Severe). Contribution D. Brown & M. Hamilton.

Beinn a Bhuird.—*Mitre Ridge*. This was the scene of several epics last winter. These experiences, together with that of Strange and King on the second winter ascent (*S.M.C.J.*, 1976, xxxi, 30) confirm the quality and character of this winter expedition and suggest the grading should be V and not IV.

Central Highlands

Creag Meaghaidh. D. Dinwoodie notes—On the 1972 ascent of *Nordwander* (*S.M.C.J.*, 1973, xxx, 182), the barrier icefall of 1959 *Face Route* was climbed directly. It was not particularly hard, and has probably had other ascents. (On the original ascent, the icefall was avoided by rocks on the right).

A. L. Wielochowski notes an ascent of the 120-ft. icicle which forms most years left of the *Direct Start* to *Ritchie's Gully*. It provided a good training route. Ice picks were used three times to rest using a sit sling. We received note of another line from Wielochowski, that line being the well-defined fault 200 ft. right of, and parallel to *Smith's Gully*. It would not be incorrect to call this line one of the last great problems. Unfortunately the manner in which this line was assaulted we find impossible to accept, and we await reports of a more digestible nature. We reproduce the following note from Wielochowski on the line. 'Poor weather made it impossible for us to complete the route in one day. On the 24th February lashing rain at midday stopped progress. Fixed ropes were left on the first pitch. On the 14th March these were used to surmount the first pitch which had lost most of its ice. The next two pitches were then climbed to *Appolyon Ledge*, gale force winds caused us to traverse off. Three days later the top three pitches were climbed. This "gully" should be in condition whenever *Smith's Gully* is in good condition, it would then provide a first class ice climb.

'The lower 300 ft. of the route were not climbed. As this section does sometimes ice over, it will, no doubt, provide some extremely steep, exposed, badly protected and very sustained, hard ice climbing some day. The first few feet of the fault, unless banked up, may require artificial techniques. This artificial section has in fact been climbed to the start of the fault proper.'

We will only add that we think siege tactics out of place in Scotland; the fact that Wielochowski's party had a total climbing time of ten hours would substantiate this. We also confess to the original sin of accepting the Clough ascent of *Point Five Gully* as a valid ascent—the present editors would not.

Newtonmore: Creag Dubh: Main Face.—*Hungarian Hamstring—Variation.* This took the 50 ft. overhanging crack above the mid point ledges. It was predictably strenuous and was climbed by R. Baillie & M. Burrows-Smith, June 1976.

Ordan Shios. This is a small outcrop south of Newtonmore on the Insh road (G.R. 96 71). About a dozen routes, averaging 100 ft. in length and of a Very Difficult-Severe nature were found by E. Henderson. He points out that the outcrop stands on private grounds, and permission had to be obtained.

Glen Nevis: Buzzard Crag. A. L. Wielochowski notes—This is not part of Polldubh Crags proper, it lies about 1 km downstream, 10-15 minutes from the road (G.R. 144 693). The crag is the lower of a pair of reddish crags seen clearly when going up the glen. On first acquaintance it appears unclimbable, but the rock is excellent and of a different character from that of the Polldubh Crags. Exploration began at least as early as 1963, and there are some good pitches to be found.

Glencoe

Buachaille Etive Mór: The Restless Earth. P. Hodgkiss notes—Following an ascent of *The Chasm*, in July 1976. 'Shortly above the Red Wall (pitch 5), there used to be a problem in the form of an easy, but very wet staircase, of some 30 ft., hard against the true right wall. This space has now been sub-let to a huge boulder which appears to have flitted from the blind south fork above. The tenant is about 20 ft. across and completely blocks the gully: there is no straightforward way over the obstacle and the easiest bypass found was up the true right wall, approximately 50 ft. back from the boulder, where an open, greasy corner of 30 ft. was climbed at about Severe.'

Great Gully Upper Buttress. W. Todd notes an ascent of the crack line 30 ft. left of *Yam*. This was first climbed by I. Nicholson but never recorded. It was found to be as good as, and slightly harder than *Yam*. *Yamay* was climbed without the original three peg runners and is well protected using modern gear.

On **Slime Wall**, *Apocalypse* was climbed without its aid peg and using a more logical third pitch. Pitch three—step right and climb shallow groove to below steep wall, traverse right to belay on *Apparition*.

Southern Highlands

Arrochar: The Cobbler. J. Hutchinson notes an ascent of *Ithuriel's Wall* with no aid. The route as such is Hard Very Severe.

Dunkeld: Craig-y-Barns: Free at Last. We note the following routes now climbed with no aid—*Left Hand Crack, The Corpse, Squirm' Squirm Direct, Rat Catcher, Hang Out, The Civer* (one peg as hold), and *The Stank*. All these routes, of course, are at least Very Severe. The last named route has been free-climbed for some time now, and provides a good second pitch to *The Civer*. *The Civer* climbed as above is probably the hardest pitch at Craig-y-Barns.

Haddington: Traprain Law. *Dangle* and *Hanging Crack* have been climbed free for some time now, and recently *Beatle Crack* has been freed of all aid to give one of the hardest routes on the crag. We are indebted to Messrs. Cuthbertson, Hamilton and Taylor for being so free with their information, and would add that, if as rumoured, a group are in the process of updating the Creag Dubh and Eastern Outcrops Guide, they communicate directly with the Editor, who can supply fuller information than can be given here.

THE LAST POINT

Adherents of (to?) the Finnieston Railway Wall, Glasgow, will be dismayed to learn that workmen are at present pointing the cracks in the wall. The spread of bureaucracy has not gone unnoticed in the past; looking grimly into the future one can see holds being buffed off classic routes, gullies being filled in, and the hills themselves being levelled out. There is no room for complacency.

MISCELLANEOUS NOTES

Monroölogy: Theory.—H. M. Brown contributes the following useful account of the remoter 3000-foot summits of the British Isles:

FURTH OF SCOTLAND

This is the term used for the 3000-foot summits in Wales, Ireland and England to balance our own real home-brewed Munros. There has always been a certain amount of confusion, largely with the Irish ones, but the answer is simple: you do everything to make sure! To date only 25 people have done the Scottish Munros, Tops, and all the minutiae Furth of Scotland. This suggests that common among the remaining Munro-baggers is a lack of thoroughness, an untidy mind or a self-punishing nationalism. There are some good things to be found 'ootwith wir ain baick yaird,' especially in Ireland where the hills are like our own and the O.S. even worse.

D. C. Maxwell compiled Tables in line with Munro's which are likely to be as definitive as anything else. There is not much debate over the English and Welsh listings but in Ireland various lists had been done and as their O.S. only give a couple of names on the fine ridge of the Macgillycuddy's Reeks (the best ridge outside Skye?) you can even make up names if you like. Much checking was done by the late Willie Docharty and published in his three tomes. Maxwell has built on these and my only complaint is that he reduces the 3000'ers to two in the Reeks by keeping to stringent definitions which we have never had for our Munros. This most un-Irish approach is a pity. But only a fool will miss anything in the Reeks. Caher, which appears in no list, has the narrowest ridge in all the four countries—and a shrine on top. For Munro-worshippers who would delve deeper in these mysteries S.M.C.J., 1968, *xxix*, 39, mentions several articles on this theme.

Anyway, for the benefit of Munroists who have taken my first paragraph to heart and are extra-murally inclined, here is the *Furth of Scotland* list.

WALES

8 'Munros' and 6 Tops in 3 groups—The Carnedds, The Glyders and Snowdon.

	Order of Altitude	Height		Map Reference
		Feet	Metres	
Carnedd Llywelyn	2	3485	1065	684645
Foel-grach	–	3196	974	688649
Yr-elen	–	3152	961	673652
Carnedd Dafydd	3	3425	1044	663631
Penyrole-wen	–	3211	979	656620
Foel-fras	6	3091	942	697682
Glyder Fawr	4	3279	999	642580
Glyder Fach	–	3262	994	657583
Y Garn	5	3104	946	631595
Elidir Fawr	7	3030	924	612613
Tryfan	8	3008	917	663594
Yr Wyddfa	1	3560	1085	610544
Carnedd Ugain	–	3495	1065	611552
Crib Goch	–	3023	921	627553

Maps: O.S. 1 inch, Sheet 107 and O.S. 1:50,000, Sheet 115.

IRELAND

5 'Munros' and 6 Tops according to Maxwell, or
8 'Munros' and 5 Tops according to Brown

	Order of Altitude	Height		Map Reference	
		Feet	Metres		
Lugnaquilia	7	3039	926	T 030916 Sheet 16	The highest of the rolling Wicklow Mountains south of Dublin.
Galtymore	8	3018	920	R 879240 Sheets 17 & 21	The highest of the Galty Mountains between Tipperary and Mitchelstown. Good traversing.
Brandon Mountain	5	3127	953	Q 464117 Sheet 20	The furthest west 3000'er, a splendid peak on the Dingle Peninsula. Best from the North.

Macgillycuddy's Reeks (which must be good with a name like that! Situated near Killarney in the South West—all on Sheet 20)

Carrauntoohil	1	3414	1041	V 804844	
Beenkeragh*	2	3314	1010	V 802853	¾ m N.N.W. of 1
Cahernaveen*	3	3285	1001	V 795838	¾ m W.S.W. of 1
Cummeenapeasta	4	3260	994	V 836841	2 mls E.S.E. of 1
Barrabwee	–	3185	971	V 828834	⅝ m S.W. of 4
Knockacuillion	–	3141	957	V 823832	1 m S.W. of 4

Crom Cruach* 6	3110	948	V 841845	¼ m N.E. of 4
Cruach –	3062	933	V 841848	½ m N.N.E. of 4
(Caher –	3200	975	V 790840	¼ m West of Cahernaveen)
(Knockoughter –	3140	957	V 801847	¼ m S. of Beenkeragh)

Maps: Irish O.S. ½ inch

The last two are omitted by Maxwell and those marked * deserve to be given the full Munro status, as they would if on the Glen Shiel ridge.

As can be seen, collectors of Donaldsons have a very easy time Furth of Scotland, there being only three in Ireland and three in Wales, although prudence would dictate the inclusion of Glyder Fawr as a borderline case.

At the end of September 1977, I hope to be motoring over to revisit all the Irish 3000'ers again and would be glad to hear from any Munro-baggers interested in joining in.

ENGLAND

4 'Munros' and 3 Tops	Order of Altitude	Height Feet	Metres	Map Reference
Scafell Pikes	1	3206	977	215072
Broad Crag	–			219076
Ill Crags	–			223074
Scafell	2	3162	964	207064
Helvellyn	3	3116	950	341151
Lower Man	–	3033	924	338155
Skiddaw	4	3054	931	260291

Maps: O.S. 1 inch, Sheets 82 and 83, and O.S. 1:50,000, Sheet 90.

Munroölogy: Practice.—We have received the following reports of people who have completed the revised list of Munros:

(125) M. G. Geddes, 1970, 1970, —;   (135) R. Payne, 1976, —, —;
(126) J. Gillies, 1971, —, —;   (136) W. Douglas, 1976, —, —;
(127) W. C. T. Sarson, 1973, 1973, —;   (137) M. Keates, 1976, —, —;
(128) A. L. Mackenzie, 1973, —, —;   (138) E. Pilling, 1976, —, —;
(129) L. Mackenzie, 1975 — —;   (139) R. Morgan, 1976, 1976, —;
(130) K. R. Cox, 1976, —, —;   (140) A. E. Law, 1976, —, —;
(131) C. Marsden, 1976, —, —;   (141) D. Tooke, 1976, —, —;
(132) D. Hunter, 1976, —, —;   (142) R. Graham, 1976, —, —;
(133) R. L. St.C. Murray, 1976, —, —;   (143) Murdo E. Macdonald, 1977, —,
(134) I. C. Spence, 1976, —, —;   —;

(75) Matthew Moulton has done both Munros and Tops for a second time. (119) R. Hardie should be corrected to read 1974, 1976, 1976 and (121) C. W. Turner, 1973, 1973, —. The list, of course, is provisional. One day the records will be examined in detail and the correct sequence of completing will be worked out. However, the recent wave of Ordnance Survey orogenesis sweeping the West Highlands may be a continuing phenomenon and Munroists will have to top up every year in order to keep up with the Munros.

The Call of the Hills.—In our last issue we printed an article on the water of life in bath, bottle and glass by the bibulophile Ogilvie. This has struck a chord somewhere in Grid Reference 039847. An anonymous correspondent from this airt inspired by Ogilvie's success and having an equal talent for fundamental research disputes the description of the J.M.C.S. Glasgow Section War Cry given by the Section's Official Historian in a previous issue of the *Journal* and seeks to settle the score by placing this important utterance on a sounder musicological basis.

He writes—'We are indebted to your scientific researcher Iain H. Ogilvie for his spirited article in *S.M.C.J.*, 1976, *xxi*, 46. At what stage, we would all like to know, does alcoholic evaporation allow us to handle the *Journal* without wetting the covers? And when does the wet-cold spiral begin?

You cannot be blamed for the editorial blemishes in previous *Journals*. These are squarely laid on your unmusical predecessor. However, I must correct the inaccuracy in *S.M.C.J.*, 1975, *xxx*, 330, *line* 5. The Juniors were never minors. The J.M.C.S. cry is a MAJOR third progressing melodically from mediant to tonic like most good cuckoos. (Some cuckoos at grid reference 039847 are so overcome by inertia that their third is flattened by almost a semitone, but this is hardly relevant). A rope of three would find it very effective to sing in close harmony the second inversion of any major triad (which is resonant enough to reach the C.I.C. hut in any weather). Ideally our bass sings the fifth of the triad, our baritone the root or tonic and our tenor the mediant or third. The triad of A major provides a comfortable tessitura: the bass singing E, the baritone A and the tenor C sharp.

'With a little practice a rope of three should perfect this harmonious exercise, the tenor leading, the baritone in the middle and the bass stamping in the spindrift. A tuning-fork will help to fix the pitch. Experts will want to practice the pitch at the crux. (Graham Tiso might consider manufacturing a piton hammer tuned to an A. It is awkward extracting an oboe from a rucsack on the crux, and the reed is likely to be cold. No respectable orchestra tunes to a recorder). Former editors and other unmusical people would be better not to try but just to carry whistles. Middle-aged members of the J.M.C.S. may remember practicing this exercise in the Lofoten Islands in imitation of the hooters on the Norwegian coastal steamers.

'Yodelling, of course, is a sophisticated one-man major triad, when it isn't a dominant seventh. Meistersingers should compete for the Sang Award.'

The author of this tract which must surely be incomprehensible to anyone short of a B.Mus. has, not surprisingly, concealed his identity from all except the most persevering cartographic detectives by giving a Grid Reference without Grid Letters.

J.M.C.S. Jubilee Dinner Photograph

Know Thyself.—Jim Messer writes: 'I received the following additions and alterations to the list of people attending the J.M.C.S. Jubilee Dinner in the Central Hotel, Glasgow, on Saturday, 11th October, 1975. Only three people wrote in by the time I left Glasgow therefore I assume the missing faces are keen to maintain their anonymity or were suffering from alcoholic amnesia. It would be interesting if we could identify all present as there are still twenty-one heads not named. The updated list is as follows:—

No. 85—Guthrie Strang.   No. 67—Peter Myles.   No. 79—Alex Dunn.
No. 36—Douglas Steven.   No. 77—Ian Brodie.   No. 95—David More.

'J. Logan Aikman wrote to me saying that No. 125 was R. W. Martin and not P. A. Fletcher as stated, he also felt that he may be No. 144 as he was standing with W. B. Speirs to his right.

'If anyone else can help to identify the missing faces they should write to me c/o I.G.A., St. Anthony, AOK 4SO, Newfoundland, Canada.'

LETTERS TO THE EDITOR

The Bureaucracy Debate

SIR—At the last Annual General Meeting of the Club we were asked to approve a motion that the Club give its support to the Mountaineering Council of Scotland in approaching the Scottish Sports Council for financial assiatance. Those present grued and boked for ten minutes or so and then approved the motion by a large majority. Later at the Annual Dinner our guest speaker from South of the Border gave us as plain warning as he could that a great beast of bureaucracy had been born in Manchester and was gathering its strength to lurch its way northward. We gathered that all good and true mountaineers in South Britain were wringing their hands in despair and wondering whether to flee or submit—a sort of post-Hastings situation.

Clearly something is going on and I write in the hope of stimulating some thought and even agreement on how to deploy our defences. Fortunately in Scotland we now have had ample warning and still have a breathing space in which to make our strategic and tactical dispositions.

I think the first principle to establish is that Mountaineering and Mountaineering Bureaucracy are two different sports. The concern of the Mountaineering Clubs is with Mountaineering, that is with the fellowship of those who are concerned with the metaphysics of the irreversible move and the aesthetics of the mist cascading into the Garbh Coire Mor in the darkening of a winter's evening. I think it would be a fundamental strategic mistake for the Clubs to be concerned with counter-bureaucracy operations any more than they can help. It would be wrong, for example, for the Scottish Mountaineering Club to expand its membership so it could 'speak for Scottish Mountaineering' as many utopians have suggested. This would be to change a rather unique and eccentric fellowship into just another pressure group created in the image of the bureaucracy it was supposed to be resisting. This applies to all spontaneously generated clubs each of which has evolved its own identity and peculiarities over the years. The example of the Sierra Club in California should be noted. It has changed from a fellowship of mountaineers to an efficient environmental protection agency and is very nearly a political organisation. It does a very useful job but has changed its purpose. I think this very necessary role should be performed in Scotland by the M.C. of S.

Our main danger seems to be from the big population centres where there are Avogadro's number of mountaineers supporting a growing cadre of ambitious bureaucrats who, alas, have pitifully few mountains to administer—hence, as our guest speaker repeatedly warned us, the coming *Drang nach Norden* for *Berglebensraum*. Here the mountaineering community of Scotland has a common interest to deflect this dreadful *Drang* somewhere else. This includes our own bureaucrats who, while no doubt quite willing to crat us, are as averse as the next person to being cratted themselves, and this is what would happen to them in any final Pan-British solution. Among the refugee climbers presently fleeing northwards there is a greater awareness of the danger than among us naive natives and they tend to be more fervently northern than ourselves.

I suggest that our best strategy is summarised in the fable of the Dog, the Lapwing and the Roebuck which states in mythographic terms the only practical solution to this type of problem. The clubs must emulate the roebuck, invisible in the thickets to all but discerning eyes. The role of the M.C. of S. is twofold, to emulate the lapwing, distracting predators away from the clubs and the secret places among the mountains and to be the guardian watch dog, an intelligent hound that fixes its teeth into the heels of ambitious bureaucrats.

Although I voted against the proposal, after due thought I feel that the situation is so serious that the M.C. of S. needs all the help it can get and that, provided we remember our compass bearing, government money need not corrupt us. After all, the Viet Cong by all accounts were largely armed and supplied by the Americans but remained steadfastly unaffected by their political views. Yours etc.

I. H. M. SMART.

SIR—Grateful though I am for the somewhat belated support given by Iain Smart at the end of his letter, I should like to try to clear up some misconceptions which he, and probably others, appear to hold.

As an ex-member of the B.M.C. Management Committee I have heard no suggestion that the B.M.C. might lurch its way northward. The M.C. of S. understanding with the B.M.C. is excellent. From first hand experience of the B.M.C. in action I am satisfied their policy is well thought out, very democratic and is operated by the minimum of so-called bureaucracy necessary for effective results. A colossal amount of work is done by volunteers who are dedicated mountaineers. The amateurs control the policy and the professional staff earn their bread.

Your correspondent, no doubt with tongue in cheek, sounds typical of those people who stand apart claiming to be true mountaineers, i.e. love mountains, climb well, and have nothing to do with committees and such like talking shops. Generalising is never safe but if there is another camp I must be in it—I love mountains, but climb poorly and seem to get involved in talking shops. It is only when one becomes involved one finds the pressures threatening us are a reality. The pressures on the B.M.C. and M.C. of S. are just not understood by most climbers who are interested mainly in their own rope. I don't blame them. The problems were only revealed to me when I started to look and listen.

The threats are against our free choice in respect of the routes we may walk, crags we may climb, times we may go, equipment we take or leave behind, where we may stop to sleep and the weather conditions in which we climb. The M.C. of S. is dealing with problems on each of these headings. If no volunteers are found to do this I suggest that on some weekend in the future, before climbing one might have to first contact the weather centre where the Police (no offence, Officer) have laid down minimum temperature and maximum wind speed for safety. Luckily the avalanche risk is only 0.3 so climbing is permitted, if one has an MLC (W), of course. You have! (Why?) Next one checks with the S.L.F. which estates are open (not shooting/breeding grouse, counting/culling/stalking stags/hinds, gathering sheep/cattle, lambing/calving, resting the ground or just fed up with climbers). One then checks with the Countryside Commission for Scotland to see which L.D.R's are over-booked or not open due to bothy redecoration. The R.S.P.B. man advises that the Lesser Spotted Chargar has returned to shit, spit, sit, so the crag is closed. 'Wild camping' is not allowed anyway on safety grounds and one will (one is told) be much happier in the new camp site under the motorway flyover (out of the rain). It's a pity its next to the new pleasure helicopter pad but the noise gives one warning when to hang on to the tent. In any case, the local M.R. teams are running speed trials in co-operation with the local education authority who are having a 'Go to hills' weekend for the Primary fives. One might as well stay at home and read 'I Chose to Climb Down' (before I was kicked out) by the late Hon. Sec. of M.C. of S.

Fortunately there are people of good sense in all the bodies relating to the above possibilities but we still need an M.C. of S. to make sure that they are properly informed on mountaineers and their needs. Ridiculous rule-making is often born of ignorance. Where there is a genuine conflict of interest then

Photo: Hamish M. Brown

Ireland has our furthest west 3000 ft. summit—Brandon Mountain on the Dingle Peninsula

Photo: D. J. Bennet

The Post Dinner Meet—The morning after the night before on Meall Corranaidh
looking to Meall nan Tarmachan   December 1976

our rivals are likely to have bigger and better guns than we and our own youthful and amateur bureaucracy is going to need all the support we can give it.

It is a bit insulting to refer to Mountaineering Bureaucracy as a separate sport. (Of course we all do this to the M.R. folk anyway). It does reveal a lack of knowledge of the facts and a head-in-the-sand attitude, though we should remember the ostrich does that in order to hear if his mate is around so he obviously knows the facts. I hope the S.M.C. will never attempt to be 'the voice of mountaineering in Scotland.' Such would be thoroughly presumptous and as a member I should resist it, even though our Club does occupy a rather special place amongst clubs. The voice of mountaineering in Scotland is a chorus of many and the M.C. of S. tries to find a harmony and a clarity the audience can understand, no easy task considering the highly individualistic nature of most mountaineers.

The M.C. of S. is wholly democratic; the Executive Committee is elected—currently six are members of the S.M.C.—to serve the membership. Any expansion is not self interest, it means more voluntary work so it is born of necessity to meet increasing pressures. Surely the answer for those who are apprehensive about the M.C.S. is not to turn away but to involve themselves so that they influence its policies. The real danger lies in apathy leading to the M.C.S. executive becoming isolated from the membership and its consensus. Therefore, we must not allow any mountaineering hierarchy to develop—debunking is good for the soul! Others did better work before us and will do better after us.

If there is danger from the south be assured the M.C. of S. is resisting some southern ideas (not necessarily from the B.M.C.)—registration of rights of way, National Parks, one U.K. Leadersuip Training Board, one U.K. Mountaineering Council, access agreements, that helicopter again, L.D.R's, etc. Presumably this resistance is what is meant by 'bureaucracy.' 'Bureaucratic' is usually intended as a derogatory adjective. There are no bureaucrats in the M.C. fo S. in the sense of seeking control over their fellow climbers. There are a bunch of mountaineers of varying talents trying to do a job for other mountaineers and perhaps the public too. I am glad there are plenty of anti-bureaucrats in mountaineering ready to deflate any presumptiousness in M.C. of S. I am sorry there are some short sighted, blinkered mountaineers who think there will always be mountaineering in Scotland, as we know it, without effort on our part to protect it. I hope they are right and we who see a more threatening vision are wrong.

None of the Executive Committee of M.C. of S. wants the Council. We should be happy to disband it tomorrow if the roebucks and lapwings had any chance of influencing the predators before the thicket was cut down and the nest destroyed by some authority hell bent on development. The Coruisk Affair, a fight we lost, showed how our random bleating and flapping of wings was ignored. It was then I moved we scrap the A.S.C.C. and set up a body that would work in today's situation. Others obviously felt the same. I do not think any of the M.C. of S. want to emulate the infrastructure (get with the lingo man) of the Sierra Club—except in respect of their success. Our joy is a day on the hill and our interest in an M.C. of S. is so that we may continue to enjoy other days like it in the future. Yours etc.

                                                           A. G. COUSINS.

SIR—There is a welcome agreement on fundamentals between a conscientious objector like myself and a front-line fighter like Mr Cousins and in according me the courtesy of a reply I would like to try to strengthen this common ground between all unregimented mountaineers.

Mountaineers are not divided into competent purists and accident-prone committee men. Most of the latter known to me manage to get to the hills oftener than I do and never figure in the accident reports. The worry we all have about the spread of regimentation does, alas, tend to get projected against all bureaucrats whether they are freedom fighters on our side or not. Gratitude to those who give up their spare time for committee work is not one of our virtues.

Neither are mountaineers divided into age groups as the writer of the A.G.M. Report (p. 211) suggests for I saw high ranking Paedocrats and seedy Gerontocrats voting on each side of the division referred to in the opening paragraph of my first letter.

That mountaineering and mountaineering bureaucracy are different sports is not an insult but a statement of fact. The particular skills that get you up a buttress are not those that help you to deflect a committee from doing something dreadful, although both may require the same general qualities of intelligence, self control, tenacity, and all the rest of it. The plea in my first letter is for the development of a strategy that we all understand, so that every paedocrat, gerontocrat, counter bureaucrat and conscientious objector knows where he fits in and can make his contribution at the tactical level.

The important points of general agreement are:

1. that the clubs should remain as our base area concerning themselves with the aesthetics and practice of actual mountaineering and with the transmission of the true mysteries down the generations. This last, the securing of a fourth dimensional link is of major importance. For example, some of the idealistic organisations which once encouraged people to enjoy the freedom of the hills have been so successful that their function has had to change from promotion to control; they are now restricting the very freedom they once encouraged people to find. This point was raised as an objection to the M.C. of S. accepting government money—that while the present body might use it for counter-bureaucratic operations, our future representatives might well think their main role was to qualify for more and more government grants, adjust themselves accordingly and thereby incur the deadly Sadim curse[1]. Somehow if we are to secure our future we must bridge the paedo-gerontocrat[2] gap, lest in moments of doubt and confusion we forget to pass on the correct compass bearing.

2. that the force driving the bureaucratic advance against us is the pressure of numbers and that a major task of the Mountaineering Council of Scotland is to deflect this pressure elsewhere. Deflection implies a resistance in one direction and a freedom to expand in another. This was appreciated by the leadership of the Great Guerilla Confederation which won the second battle of Mons Graupius against the Roman road through the Lairig Ghru. You remember their leader's memorable, if somewhat taciturn, eve-of-battle speech, 'They will channel us in hundreds along sign-posted ways and call it access.' The opposition to the Grampian Way was intelligently deployed and at the same time the need for pedestrian ways in other locations was stressed.

3. More generally we can deflect pressure by reorganising our publicity. In this field, although possibly not everyone will agree, we have been our own worst enemy. We have written compellingly well about mountaineering in a style calculated to sell to the biggest audience, have advertised ourselves in lectures and films and have even lobbied the media into turning our activities into a spectator sport. We have conveyed with evangelical zeal the impression that mountaineering is the very champagne of life and have even made the uproariously funny suggestion that mountaineering is good for the character. If we slackened off on all these initiatives we would help to decrease the pressure on that environment from which we draw inspiration. Who can blame people for actually believing the myths we propogate so convincingly.

Where is the deflected pressure to go? In these days of cheap charter flights the cost in time and money of travelling by a well-organised charter system from a big population centre to the Alps might well be less than going to the Cuillins. Here we have an unexploited niche into which people and even a bureaucracy could expand. Yours etc.

I. M. M. SMART.

Footnotes:

1. The Sadim curse is the Midas curse in reverse; everything touched turns into lead.

2. A *gerontocrat* is someone ten years older than yourself, a *paedocrat* is ten years younger. These periods may be reduced to five years if you are really strongly opposed to someone else's views. The division (unlike the one between the Salvationist-Ultramontane) is not valid. Paedocrats are gerontocrats-in-waiting and very briefly at that. Nevertheless you can feel the frosty autumn fingers closing on your heart when you hear for the first time your boyish idealism being dismissed as the rigid attitude of a gerontocrat. *Eheu fugaces.*

EDITOR'S NOTE—We trust that potential *Journal* contributors will appreciate that what Dr Smart is really advocating in his penultimate paragraph is that those who are compelled by hard economic necessity to write for the commercials and glossies should turn their talents to writing 'compellingly well' about anything *except* mountaineering. Such articles on this subject should of course continue to be presented for the cognoscenti in the pages of this and other club journals.

THE SCOTSMAN — OUTDOOR PARTY INFORMATION SHEET

1. FILL OUT **ALL** THE DETAILS ON **BOTH** SIDES OF THIS SHEET AND HAND IT TO A RESPONSIBLE PERSON, WHO WILL IN TURN FORWARD IT TO THE **POLICE** IN THE EVENT OF YOU BEING OVERDUE.

2. **REMEMBER** TO INFORM THE RESPONSIBLE PERSON IMMEDIATELY YOU RETURN.

Time and Date of Setting out.	Estimated Time and Date of Return / Completion.	Map being used by Party:— Sheet No.— Scale—	Did you check on Local Weather Forecasts. Yes ☐ No ☐	Local Police Phone No.

The Party is composed of .... Leaders and .... Party members, and will be involved in:-- *(Tick Box)* ☑

ROCK CLIMBING		SNOW – ICE CLIMBING		HILLWALKING— SUMMER		HILLWALKING— WINTER		SKI - ING	

Give complete details of all members of the Party— Name, Age, Experience, Address, Phone No., Next of Kin.

If you run out of space use second sheet.

NAME—
AGE—
EXPERIENCE—
ADDRESS—
PHONE No.—
NEXT OF KIN—

NAME—
AGE—
EXPERIENCE—
ADDRESS—
PHONE No.—
NEXT OF KIN—

NAME—
AGE—
EXPERIENCE—
ADDRESS—
PHONE No.—
NEXT OF KIN—

NAME—
AGE—
EXPERIENCE—
ADDRESS—
PHONE No.—
NEXT OF KIN—

NAME—
AGE—
EXPERIENCE—
ADDRESS—
PHONE No.—
NEXT OF KIN—

Give exact details of your route and objectives, including map references for each.

Escape Route No. 1.

Escape Route No. 2.

TO.. OF..
the details of our Party are as listed on this Form   Should we fail to check-in by....................on....................day
the....................of....................19....... would you please make this Sheet available to the Police.

.... *Party Leader.*

IMPORTANT:-- (a) Fill out in detail the reverse of this sheet.
(b) Remember to check-in with the responsible person.

Devised by **COLIN YELLAND** -- Glenshee Ski Rescue Service.

ALL THE MEMBERS OF THE PARTY SHOULD HAVE ADEQUATE CLOTHING AND FOOTWEAR. IF THIS IS SO PUT A TICK IN THE BOX. PUT THE AMOUNT OF SPECIALISED EQUIPMENT CARRIED BY THE PARTY BELOW.

MAP(S)	ROPE(S)	SLEEPING BAG(S)	SPARE SWEATER(S)	SPARE SOCK(S)
TORCH(ES)	ICE AXE(S)	TENT(S)	SPARE BATTERIE(S)	PITON(S)
COMPASS(ES)	CRAMPON(S)	DUVET(S)	HAMMER(S)	BALACLAVA(S) HELMET(S)
WHISTLE(S)	FIRST-AID KIT(S)	FLASK(S)	CAGOULE TOP(S)	GLOVE(S)
FLARE(S)	BIVVI BAG(S) or SHEET(S)	SURVIVAL FOOD(S)	CAGOULE TROUSER(S)	RUCKSACK(S) / HAVERSACK(S)

As a rough guide in assessing Outdoor Experience put a cross on the line indicating degree of experience.

e.g.—Inexperienced... I ....X................... very experienced.

LEADERS | PARTY MEMBERS

Inexperienced........................I...................very experienced | Inexperienced.......................I.......................very experienced

If very experienced — How many years so?.............................

Give details of any member of the party who is liable to suffer from any specific medical complaint: also give details of any special medicines carried:—

Address at which party is staying in the area:—

Description and exact location Group's Transport will be left at during excursion:—

Registration Number(s):—

If the party is from a School or Youth Organisation, please give details of the person to contact in the event of the party being overdue:—

Any other relevant information:—

IMPORTANT — REMEMBER TO CHECK-IN WITH WHOEVER HAS THE FORM !

For you—
For Scotland

ALTHOUGH THIS FORM IS SUPPLIED FREE BY "THE SCOTSMAN", LOCAL RESCUE TEAMS WOULD BE DELIGHTED TO RECEIVE SMALL DONATIONS FROM PARTIES WISHING TO MAKE THEM.

Bureaucracy Rampant—Attention all Ostriches

As a warning of the kind of thought processes emerging over the peripheral rim of the mountain world we reproduce a form recently published by a national newspaper (which whould know better). We hasten to add that it has no connection with or approval from the Mountain Rescue Committee for Scotland—or the M.C. of S.

Don't bother to count; we already have, and can tell you that the conscientious party should fill up 153 spaces before setting out. Take heart however, if there are only three in your group you can get by with only 87.

On the other hand we should perhaps regard such productions as being in accordance with Smart's penultimate paragraph, in that anyone seriously contemplating its completion is unlikely to retain the tenacity and strength to actually set out on the hills.

SCOTTISH MOUNTAIN ACCIDENTS, 1976

As USUAL, the 1976 Accident Report has been compiled and sent to us by B. H. Humble. Sadly, it is the last we shall receive from his pen, as Ben died this spring. Accident reports will never be the same again and we shall all miss the characteristic Humble turn of phrase with its references to 'smooth soled shoes' and 'the simple slip.' It is to be hoped that a successor will emerge who will continue the difficult task Ben performed so enthusiastically over so many years. In our view this is a valuable service which should not be allowed to lapse.

1976 M.R.C.S. Accident Survey Extract

'Reports indicate a continued increase in the number of both hill walkers and climbers on our hills in 1976 and particularly teenage, school and Youth Organisation parties. Many of the latter are now being sent on lesser hills, such as the Ochils, the Trossachs area and the Kilpatricks. Even on these hills weather can be severe at times, particularly in winter. There is, of course, always an element of risk and many of the accidents are of a minor nature, often due to a simple slip, often unavoidable. One school party were sent on a two-day expedition involving an overnight camp. It proved too arduous for them and they managed off the hills in an exhausted condition well short of their objective just as Rescue parties were alerted. The report states they had had but one previous day expedition, two days classroom instruction in map reading and no instruction in how to erect a tent.

'In Glencoe the Lost Valley path, perhaps because of its name has become something of a magnet for hill walkers and can be very icy under winter conditions, the same applying to tourist path up Ben Nevis.

'In the north side of the Cairngorms from the summer of 1977 there will be an automatic relay service from Glenmore Lodge giving immediate Weather Reports. The Countryside Commission for Scotland also operates a Ranger Service at the upper car park with information and advice for would-be hill walkers. There is now very close co-operation between the Police, the experienced staff of Glenmore Lodge, Chairlift Staff, Cairngorm M.R.T., R.A.F. and Helicopters and Dr Neil McDonald, resulting in very speedy evacuations under difficult conditions.

'There were some thirteen call-outs for people overdue or erroneously reported missing. It must be emphasised that well equipped and experienced climbers can and do withstand a night out even in the most severe winter conditions and are none the worse in the morning. (Did not Haston and Scott spend a night out near summit of Everest?) Almost inevitably however friends and relatives become anxious and search parties alerted or called out. Experienced climbers always try and mostly do, get back as early as possible the next day in time to cancel a call-out but this does not usually apply to inexperienced hill walkers, particularly those of school age.

'Helicopters were called on for evacuations of many casualties and were used in almost all searches (on at least 36 call-outs—Ed.). Great credit is due to the pilots and winchmen of these craft for their fine work under most difficult conditions. Search dogs were also much used and on three occasions found missing teenagers. More than ever now our Voluntary Civilian Teams are called on by the Police for incidents not in any way connected with mountaineering or hill walking—skiers lost in mist, old and young folk lost from home, inmates lost from Mental homes, two cases of suicide on the hills, fallen fishermen, photographers and even a hang-glider (the shape of things to come).

'*Teams involved:* Dundonnel, Glenelg, Kintail, Cairngorm, Glenmore Lodge, Lochaber, Glencoe, Ochils and South Scotland plus Police teams from all the Regions, plus as always, much help from R.A.F. M.R. Teams from Leuchars and Kinloss. Army units and helicopters.'

Selected Accident List

NORTH AND WEST HIGHLANDS

JANUARY 24—*Benighted*—Lieut. Humphreys (29), Black Watch, overdue on expedition in Sutherland. Well equipped in every way and experienced. Overtaken by bad weather—heavy snow, hence bivouacked and continued his journey as soon as practicable and contacted possible search at first possible destination. Perfectly fit and well. This sort of thing occurs now and again to experienced climbers.

JULY—*False Alarm*—Glenelg and Kintail Team out on search as whistle heard from Arnisdale on face of Drum Fhada above Dubh Lochan. No one reported missing and no one found.

NEVIS AREA

FEBRUARY 2—*Snow Slip*—Gordon Kelford (19), Lancashire Police Climbing Club, while climbing on arête Coire Leis slipped, unable to stop with ice axe, fell about 200 feet. Lacerations to head and fractured arm. Police team, 10 man hours.

FEBRUARY 16—*Benighted*—R.A.F. Kinloss called to Fort William re six climbers reported overdue. Helicopter found two of them at C.I.C. hut while other four were benighted and bicouacked on top of Great Tower of Tower Ridge. Completed climb and found on plateau. All fit—no injuries. Team did not go out.

MARCH 1—Nicholas Hogg (15) with school party from Preston, with 8 other boys and two leaders, climbed Nevis by tourist path, descending via Coire Leis using abseil posts. Lost grip on rope when being lowered, slid about 80 feet. Compound fracture right leg.

MARCH 30—*Snow Slip*—Colin Owen (24), Southampton, slipped on summit of Càrn Mhór Dearg. Hard packed snow. Unable to stop with ice axe, fell about 200 feet. Severe bruising to kidneys. Evacuation by helicopter.

MARCH 30—*Snow Slip*—Michael Ledger (31), Middlesex, slipped on icy snow on Sgùrr a Mhaim (Mamores). Unable to stop with ice axe, slid about 150 feet. Fractured skull, cuts and bruising.

APRIL 4—*Rock Climb*—Paul Nixon, Plymouth, while about 60 feet up Centurion climb, Nevis, slipped and fell to base. Injuries to right foot and leg. Evacuation by helicopter.

JUNE 22—*Benighted, Lost*—Bruce Rand (35), lost himself when descending Nevis in thick mist. Got down next morning, unhurt. Helicopter called on.

JULY 8—Michael Cranfield (21), hillwalking with two others from Kinlochleven to Glen Nevis, tried to climb rock face Lower Steall Waterfall, slipped and fell. Multiple injuries. Fatal. No rock climbing experience.

GLENCOE

FEBRUARY 10—*Benighted*—Andra Roth (32) and Amanda Gurbett (21) from England, former a very experienced climber, latter 18 months experience, both very well equipped, completed climb on Stob Coire an Lochan; high winds, white-out conditions—benighted. Helicopter and teams called out at first light, girl suffering from exposure.

FEBRUARY 14—*Snow Slip*—Sheila Slatford (23) hill walker in party but with no ice axe, when traversing a slope of snow and ice slipped and slid down about 200 feet—slight head injuries. Accident at 1.40 p.m.

FEBRUARY 19—*Snow Slip*—Mary McKerrow (22) hill walker with party from Edinburgh, climbed Bidean nam Bian. Intended to return via Coire Gabhail, then decided to retrace their steps and return via Bidean. While doing so, girl slipped on hard packed snow, unable to stop with ice axe, fell about 500 feet. Fatal injuries. No crampons. Accident at 2 p.m.

FEBRUARY 21—*Snow Slip*—David Bailey (33), Derbyshire. Descending Allt Coire Gabhail, slipped and started to slide down snow slope. Tried to use ice axe to stop himself but appeared to get entangled in his clothing and unable to use it. Went over edge and fell about 400 feet. Multiple injuries—fatal.

FEBRUARY 24—*Snow Slip*—Gillian Balshaw (29), Manchester, was fixing her crampons to her boots because of hard packed snow and ice when descending from Bidean nam Bian, she overbalanced and slid down, tried to use ice axe to stop but fell about 400 feet, fall terminating in boulder field. Very high winds, heavy rain. R.A.F. Kinloss M.R.T. were in vicinity on training and with help of some members of Glencoe Team, carried her down. Owing to weather conditions and low cloud no helicopter used. She had broken rib, collapsed lung, fractured pelvis and lacerations of scalp.

JUNE 5—*Rock Climb*—David Lowe (26), Dunfermline, climbing experience, leading Ramp Pitch, Clachaig Gully, went off route and while climbing right wall at height of 60 feet, lost hand hold and fell to top of Great Cave Pitch, from where extracted. Fractured shoulder, fractured wrist, lacerations to face and skull. Raining at time of accident. Evacuation by helicopter.

NOVEMBER 7—*Rock Climb, Loose Rock*—Patrick Merrick (26) Blackpool, while climbing lower part of last pitch Clachaig Gully, it is thought he either stood on or grabbed at some loose rock which came away, resulting in his falling 20 feet. Multiple head injuries. Fatal.

SKYE

APRIL 19—Michael Carver (36), Kent.   Holder of Mountain Leadership Certificate. 16 years experience. Rock dislodged under his feet on Clach Glas. Fell 300 feet into gully. Multiple injuries. Fatal.

MAY 27—Thomas Sweeney (27), experienced climber, had finished ascent of Great Prow and was scrambling along ridge between Blaven and Clach Glas when he slipped and fell down scree into gully, fell about 100 feet. Broken leg, lacerations to face. Helicopter evacuation.

MAY 30—Michael Hall (33), Coventry. fairly experienced, was leading on Abraham's route, Sgùrr Alasdair, when about 250 feet from summit slipped on wet basalt, 40 feet from his second. Second held him but he fell about 80 feet, breaking both legs. Second sent a climber who was nearby, down to Glen Brittle for help. Leuchars M.R.T. were exercising on adjacent hills and were informed of accident by radio. Three parties converged to within 300 feet of casualty. Accident at 3 p.m. Helicopter arrived and lowered the winchman to assess the situation. Due to location of casualty the helicopter was unable to complete the rescue without assistance. Three team members were winched down to casualty at 5.45 p.m. The casualty was then prepared for a lift whilst the helicopter refuelled. At 7 p.m. the casualty was evacuated to Broadford Hospital. The helicopter then returned to evacuate the rescue party.

CAIRNGORMS AND LOCHNAGAR

JANUARY 29—*Exposure*—Three parties from Joint Services Mountain Training Centre set off on 27th when conditions fairly good. Spent night in snow holes. Weather very bad on 28th. One party returned to snow hole on

Coire Domhain, another descended to Sinclair Hut via March Burn. Third apparently unable to return to snow hole and made an emergency bivouac near cairn at summit of Fiacall a Coire Cas. During night blizzard conditions. Instructor with this party noticed Lance Corporal Vernon (25), Scarborough, suffering from exposure and went off for help. Glenmore Lodge staff, Army instructors, Chair Lift staff, Cairngorm M.R.T., helicopter and dogs all involved. Conditions atrocious, ski road blocked at Sugar Bowl with 18-feet deep drifts and worse on plateau. Vernon found dead from exposure, by Glenmore Lodge team.

MARCH 12—*Avalanche*—Trevor Axeworthy (18), Plymouth, leg and arm injuries when party avalanched on Goat Track, Coire an t'Sneachda. Other Lodge groups on Winter Mountaineering course called on to assist. A party on way to help from Coire an Lochain, group avalanched near Col Fiacall an t'Sneachda, six of the party injured. A helicopter had already been called for first incident and a second one called for the other. Full evacuation by helicopters. One man, David Hadfield, died in hospital later. Very effective helicopter and rescue procedures, all off hill by 19.40 p.m. Cairngorm M.R.T., Police and other climbers co-operated.

MARCH 13—Charles Draycup (20), Gritstone Club, experienced, was climbing in Runnel, Coire an t'Sneachda, although avalanche warnings had been given and gullies were in very dangerous condition in upper parts, with huge cornices. 70 feet above his second (no runners), Draycup came off and fell 140 feet, due to avalanche, receiving fatal injuries. He was wearing Continental type of helmet. Belay held, and his second had hand injuries. Cairngorm M.R.T. and Glenmore staff who were nearby arranged for lower. When helicopter arrived, winchman lowered and picked up body from base of gully.

MARCH 14—George Paton (20) and Peter Moffat (35), both from Inverness, climbing unroped Raeburn's Gully Lochnagar. Spindrift all the time. About 12.30 p.m. Moffat had reached the ice pitch with Paton 150 feet behind. Suddenly some solid snow came down, missing Moffat who was in an ice cave, but hitting Paton and dislodging him, and he fell to foot of climb, suffering fractured right femur. Climbers nearby gave first aid, and one set off for help to Spittal of Glen Muick, where there were some members of Braemar and Aberdeen M.R.T's. A helicopter called on, though flying conditions marginal. It was unable to effect a pick-up and landed at south end of loch. Ground party moved casualty to more favourable position and he was picked up by helicopter. Weather conditions very bad, and one member of Aberdeen M.R.T. suffered from exposure and had to be escorted back to Spittal.

JULY 19—*Cragfast*—Four Aberdeen schoolboys, all about 15, and with no experience, wearing jeans and gym shoes, climbing 125 feet rock face on Craigendarroch Hill, Ballater. Two got to top. A rock came away when third was holding on to it and he fell 80 feet to foot of crag, the rock falling on his arm. Fourth panicked and became rockfast 40 feet from top when he saw this. Braemar and Grampian M.R.T. rescued both, the third with broken wrist.

SEPTEMBER 8—*That early blizzard*—Seven Belgians, three men and four women, one of the men a doctor, were in camp at Glenmore Site. They enquired at Forestry Information Centre if there were any high level huts. The clerkess there informed them correctly there were no such huts. She enquired about equipment and clothing. They stated (very incorrectly, as was afterwards shown), that they had such. They did not mention Shelter Stone of Loch Avon. Weather fairly good in morning when they set off. None of them had proper equipment. Footgear included Hush Puppies, Wellingtons and plimsolls and clothing jeans and light trousers. They carried no extra gear and but little food. It seems they noted Shelter Stone marked on map and assumed it was an alpine type of hut. Weather deteriorated in afternoon and they arrived at Shelter Stone all cold and wet. Nothing to cook with, and no hot food. Chris Watts, an Outward Bound instructor, and girl friend were in occupation. Both very well equipped and Chris a most experienced mountaineer. The party spent a miserable night under the Stone and overnight a heavy snowfall (first of winter), almost blizzard conditions. Though none of the Belgians were in good condition their leader still wanted to return with them over Ben Macdhui. Chris had some difficulty in talking them out of it. He and his friend gave them hot drinks and realised they would have difficulty in returning and so went with them, to help. Conditions steadily grew worse and by the time they were in upper part of Coire Raibeirt they were in bad condition. Three were showing signs of exposure and one collapsed. Watts got them in to their spare sleeping bags and left them in the shelter of a snow bank. After that he and his friend had much difficulty in getting the other four over to Coire Cas, one man almost having to be dragged. Got them all safe down to car park and called on help for the three remaining ones. A helicopter was called on but could not help, due to high winds and thick mist. It required Lodge plus a dog and dog handler in case there had been heavy drifts. The party were found in poor condition and it required a very tough carry of three stretcher loads from Coire Raibeirt to car park. It seems certain that but for the chance meeting with Watts at Shelter Stone this affair may well have ended in a major tragedy like that of the six children in 1971. It also shows how often a good forenoon is followed by a sudden change of weather in afternoon.

Criticism was made that Forestry girl should have given better advice, but note—the Forestry Information Centre is for advice re Forestry area, their low level routes, and so on. They are not mountaineers.

It is suggested that there is need for liaison between the Forestry service and the Ranger service, the latter giving advice to hill walkers and mountaineers at the Upper Car Park.

CENTRAL GRAMPIANS AND OCHILS

JANUARY 3—*Snow Climbing*—Samuel Lindsay (34), Bearsden, party of four climbing Centre Gully, Ben Lui, unroped, fell about 300 feet. Fractured ribs—evacuation Glencoe, Lomond and Leuchars M.R.T's.

MARCH 14—Stephen Endicott (23), Bristol, Christine Livingstone (22), Stirling, and Iain Stokes (22), Wolverhampton. Left car park at Glen Doll Youth Hostel to walk by Moulzie, Cairn Damh and return via Jock's Road to Glen Doll, a round trip of about 10 miles. Left at 12 noon (weather forecast that day 'sleet or snow showers'). Wind East or S.E., fresh or strong, cold, maximum 4°C. In mid afternoon the girl became footsore and tired but wished to go on. On reaching Loch Esk plateau, weather broke down with very strong winds and snow. By this time the girl was becoming exhausted and in an effort to assist her the men did not realise that the wind was pushing them off course and in fact along south side of Loch Esk.

At 5.30 p.m. girl exhausted and could go no further. Endicott stayed with her while Stokes was given map and compass and went off for help. He lost himself and arrived at Glen Doll Youth Hostel on Monday, 15th, in exhausted condition at 1.15 p.m., about 20 hours later. He gave a map reference of 233793. Helicopters and police searched the area on Monday afternoon and Leuchars M.R.T. carried out a night search till 1 a.m. on 16th.

On Tuesday 16th March, Grampian Police and Braemar M.R.T. searched from north, using snow tracks, one of which fell through frozen lochan and was bogged down. Also searches from south under very severe conditions. On 17th weather worse than ever and little could be done in way of searching. On 18th conditions good and search involved many teams and civilian helpers. All air-lifted to area in one of the biggest air lifts in history of Scottish Mountain Rescue. Search dogs also called on. This time packs belonging to the missing pair were found by search dogs. Search continued and bodies found on Saturday, 20th March, under about six inches of snow. No attempt had been made to dig a snow hole. Both had plastic survival bag. It appeared that the two had not survived the first night and probably were dead even before search started.

SEPTEMBER 9—John Bond (50), Herts., experienced hill walker, climbed Ben Cruachan on his own. Seen there by others. Search for three days by various teams—not yet found. (Body found in April, 1977).

OCTOBER 18—Andrew Gold (35), Lanarkshire, Larkhall Academy Hill Walking Club, collapsed and died when climbing Ben More, Crianlarich. Coronary thrombosis.

ARROCHAR, BEN LOMOND, TROSSACHS AREA

FEBRUARY 2—Robert Taylor (49), Bishopton, inexperienced and wearing 'Tuf' boots and carrying a length of rope, went to top of a rock face about 200 yards from old Rest and Be Thankful road. Attached length of rope to an existing piton, apparently with the idea of teaching his son the rudiments of rock climbing. His son then went to foot of crag and prepared to climb back. As he started he felt himself slipping and shouted to his father to let go the rope. Son fell a few feet to the ground and sudden loss of weight on the rope seems to have made his father overbalance so that he slipped and fell to bottom of rock. Multiple injuries—Fatal.

ARRAN

MAY 31—*Abseil*—Ronald Stott (40), Manchester, and friend Mumford, climbing Pagoda Ridge of Coire Daingean face of A'Chir. Both experienced. Decided to abseil off when heavy rain started. Mumford abseiled down safely and since rope would not run freely Stott altered the belay and put rope over a rock. Rope snapped and Stott fell 50 feet and then another 150 feet tumble. Helicopter evacuated Stott who had fractured ribs, etc., and had been wearing a helmet which may have saved his life. Rope was 11mm Kermantel about 130 feet long. It was three years old and some time previously the ends were fraying and Stott cut off about 20 feet. When examined it appeared to be of good quality and in good condition. It seems that accident occurred because rope was running over or catching on a jagged piece of rock.

JUNE 2—Robert Walshaw (26), Manchester, with two friends from same area, all hill walkers, were traversing towards north end of A'Chir ridge. At this point the other two were out of sight of Walshaw, who was some distance behind. They stopped and waited for him and when he did not appear, moved back and one saw that he had fallen and was lying below. Multiple injuries. Walshaw was a member of Lancashire Teachers Climbing Club and was in good health so it seems to have been a simple slip.

AUGUST 6—Paul Barlow (20) and Peter Lee (17), both from Devon and members of Dartmoor Rescue Team. Climbing on south west face Tarr Head, Loch Ranza. Barlow fell while leading on second pitch when a piece of rock came away in his hand. Rescue by Arran M.R.T. and Police. Fractured left ankle, torn tendons and lacerations.

AUGUST 26—Arthur Coles (53), Yorkshire, experienced hill walker. Left his wife at Brodick with intention of parking his car to walk up Goat Fell, then via Saddle to Glen Rosa. Left at 2 p.m. to be back by 5.30 p.m. Did not return to car. Reported missing at 9.30 p.m. Weather dry and sunny. On 27th fruitless search by Arran M.R.T. and Police. On 28th further search with the addition of helicopter. Found on 29th on west face, 500 feet below rocky slabs, GR 987308. Fatal.

'They must be mad'—

AUGUST 15—Robert Carter (Ayr), learning to hang glide on Conic Hill, Balmaha, under instruction of Sail Wings (Scotland), crashed into hillside. Broke right leg and right ankle. Lomond M.R.T. called out. Treated casualty on hill side and evacuated by stretcher.

As a tailpiece—one good turn deserves another.

About same time team were called on by Police to evacuate an injured Alsatian dog from Ben Lomond. Five members of team evacuated dog on an improvised stretcher. This dog, a town one, suffering from heat stroke and disc trouble causing paralysis of rear legs.

SCOTTISH MOUNTAIN ACCIDENTS AND CALL-OUTS 1976

	Casualties (Fatalities in brackets)				Direct Rescues		Searches			Total Call-Outs
	Injury	Exposure	Illness	Total	Casualties	Cragfast	Lost	Overdue or Benighted	False Alarms	
Northern Highlands	2	–	–	2	2	–	–	1	4	5
Ben Nevis Area	13(1)	–	–	13(1)	13	–	–	2	–	15
Glencoe Area	15(3)	1	1	17(3)	16	–	–	2	–	18
Skye	9(1)	–	–	9(1)	9	–	–	–	–	9
Cairngorms Area	7(3)	4(1)	2	13(4)	11	1	1	3	–	16
Central Grampians and Ochils	2	3(3)	1(1)	6(4)	4	1	2	–	1	8
Arrochar and Trossachs	4(1)	3	1	8(1)	7	–	3	–	–	10
Arran	4(2)	1	1	6(2)	5	–	1	1	–	6
Southern Uplands	–	–	–	–	–	–	–	–	–	–
All Areas	56(11)	12(4)	6(1)	74(16)	67	2	7	8	5	72

Summary

The full Report contains nearly 100 items but some of these are merely alerts. Of the 84 actual Call-outs, 12 are of a non-mountaineering nature leaving 72 actual Mountain Rescue occasions. We publish about half of these as being of particular interest. As before, a statistical table has been extracted from the Report, this time separating Call-outs from actual Casualties.

Origin and nature of parties: About half from Scotland and half from beyond the Border. 12 incidents involved 'organised' groups and 29% involved people in roped parties or on recognised climbing routes.

Summer Conditions: 53% of incidents, 9 to roped parties—including 1 abseil accident and 3 attributed to loose rock.

Winter Conditions: 47% of incidents, 12 to roped parties of which 4 attributed to 'avalanche.'

Slips on Snow: 12 this year—over one-third of winter incidents and including 2 fatalities. This is a familiar situation and again we quote the M.R.C.S. Accident Survey:—'*On our higher hills it is particularly noticeable that most accidents to hill walkers in winter were due to slips on hard snow or snow-ice. This applies to a lesser extent to climbers. The Mountaineering Council of Scotland arrange weekend courses in the use of axe and crampons but although most now carry axes, many do not appear to have had enough, if any, training in their proper use. More attention to this problem would seem to be required.*'

We are indebted to the Mountain Rescue Committee for Scotland for the information which appears in this section and record our appreciation of the efforts of the Mountain Rescue Services.

IN MEMORIAM

IAIN G. JACK

SADLY, very few of the post-war generation of members knew Iain Jack. Not many months after his demobilisation as captain at the end of six years' war-time service with searchlight units, largely in North Africa, he developed multiple sclerosis; an inevitably losing battle began and was to last for thirty increasingly difficult years. Yet up until his death on 25th April last year his courageous refusal to yield an inch to his illness, his uncomplaining patience and above all his quite amazing cheerfulness reminded those who visited him of the carefree days of the early and middle thirties when his enthusiasm knew no bounds and he was at the peak of his form on rock and snow.

Living in Renfrewshire and working before the war in Glasgow, first with the Anchor Line and later with the Blue Star Line, Iain was an early member of the J.M.C.S. and a regular attender at Glasgow Section meets. Nothing pleased him better than a really tough struggle on rock (one of his leisure-time activities was teaching boxing to gang members in one of the Gorbals youth clubs run by the late Rev Cameron Peddie) and it is not surprising that he shared in one of the outstanding new routes of the time, the first direct ascent of the Devil's Cauldron, in August 1931. His companion was J. Gordon Robinson and their time for the whole of the Chasm seven hours. Joining the Club in 1933, he took part in the following year in another epic breakthrough—Route I on the Rannoch Wall, with Williams, Todd and Macphee.

Inevitably, however, it is the personal memories which crowd in most vividly now to add the details to the picture. There was, for instance, one particularly outstanding among many great days in Glen Brittle when we did a leisurely, sun-drenched Girdle of the Sròn; there was the April day, again with my brother Colin as third, when we revelled once more in superb sunshine all along the snow-crest of the Aonach Eagach. Two days running at a Cluanie Easter meet we were caught out by darkness, once in a gully high on The Saddle, once after a long day on Beinn Fhada. I had the privilege, too, of tailing along behind him on what I think was his last climb back in 1946, the Crowberry Direct.

Yet perhaps to those of us who knew Iain both during his climbing days and later, his most memorable success was the inspiring victory he achieved in the cramping confines of his wheelchair. Our sincere sympathy goes out now to his wife Lilian and their family.

C.R.S.

T. G. ROBINSON, D.L., O.B.E., T.D.

TOM ROBINSON, a member of the Club since 1929, died at the end of January 1977. His was the era just after the First World War and at that time he and his friends brought to the S.M.C. a fresh eagerness for climbing and an urge to reach the mountain tops. Like many of us who lived in the west he learned much of his early climbing skills on the Cobbler and the neighbouring tops near Arrochar. Later he got to know the rocks of Glen Coe, Arran and Skye.

On the hills he was a fast goer, probably a result of much running at his school among the Yorkshire fells. Not surprisingly therefore his forte was in long expeditions. One of these was a New Year's Day traverse of Ben Vorlich, Ben Vane and Ben Ime. It started before dawn at Ardlui and ended after dark when the party groped for the road near the Admiralty Station on Loch Long. Another such was a week-end in September 1926 when he walked from his home in Glasgow to the top of Ben Lomond and when he got back was still fresh enough to go to a friend's house for the evening.

Tom's working life was that of a timber merchant in the family business of Robinson, Dunn & Co. Ltd., of which he became Chairman until his retirement. He had many other interests and, to mention some of them, became Lord Dean of Guild of the City of Glasgow, President of the Glasgow and West of Scotland Chamber of Commerce, Chairman of the Clyde Port Authority and Convener of the Glasgow Academicals War Memorial Fund.

In the community of Milngavie where he lived he was for ten years a member of the Town Council. Many people there and elsewhere benefited from his quiet generosity of which few were aware. He liked to be with young people. He and his wife enjoyed a happy family life with three devoted sons and their children. For many years he gave much of his time and energy to the service of St. Luke's Church as their Session Clerk.

On leaving school in 1919 he joined the Territorial Army and was fully prepared at the outbreak of the last war. As Colonel of the Glasgow Highlanders he saw service in North Africa and Italy and for years thereafter was their Honorary Colonel.

After 1945 Tom still continued to climb and attended some of the Meets of the Club. Gradually his days on the hills became fewer and more of his holidays were spent on sailing or fishing expeditions. Those of us who had the privilege of being with him on the hills, cruising among the Western Isles or trying to catch trout in a Highland loch will not forget Tom and his fund of information derived from wide reading on many subjects. His absolute reliability and integrity, his friendship and sound advice, offered unassumingly with a quiet touch of humour, are memories we shall treasure.

A.G.H. and R.N.R.

JAMES C. GRANT

JIMMY joined the Perth Section of the J.M.C.S. in 1934 and during his forty-two years of membership he served the Section in every position from President to Committee Member. In the last few years, as an Honorary Member, Jimmy took upon himself the considerable task of delivering the Section's monthly circular to members in and around Perth.

However, it was in his capacity as Honorary Secretary and Treasurer of the Section for twenty years from 1938 to 1946 and again from 1954 to 1965 that Jimmy made his greatest contribution to the Section. During these years of gradual growth in mountain activity, Jimmy was the fulcrum of meet activity and organisation.

A dedicated hill-walker, Jimmy completed his Munros in 1959 and those 'furth' of Scotland in 1961. Jimmy had also claimed 140 of the Corbetts which he had reserved for his unhappily all too brief retirement. Only last year Jimmy realised one of his life's ambitions by walking the Pennine Way and he had plans to follow this with the Coast to Coast Walk from St. Bees Head to Robin Hood's Bay this year.

However, it was not only his love of hill-walking which took Jimmy into the countryside but also his interest in photography, ornithology and latterly geology. The result of this was that the mention of a place-name from any corner of Scotland elicited the recounting of an incident or a point of interest from the locality.

Jimmy, throughout his many years of membership, was a regular attender on Section meets and could always provide information on the most interesting and usually the least strenuous route up a hill. Saturday evenings on Section meets were filled by the good-humoured raillery of Jimmy's customary hard-fought game of Canasta.

Jimmy worked for many years in the offices of the *Perthshire Advertiser*. He was also very active in the organisation of the Perthshire Society of Natural Science and rarely did a year go by without Jimmy presenting a lecture to the Society on any one of a variety of subjects.

His sudden death on 1st October was a great shock to his many friends and all of us will miss Jimmy's knowledgeable conversation and ready humour which made him a first-class companion to have on the hills. We extend our deepest sympathy to his wife and son.

J.W.R.

DOUGAL HASTON — CUMHA DUGHALL

So, mighty Haston, the painter of Lagangarbh, has gone now, too: killed in some meaningless ski-ing accident. It's worst when they die abroad. Remember the aching disbelief when Smith went, the dreams from which you couldn't bear to wake, the feeling that you'd turn a corner, somewhere near the High Street, and there he would be—tatty raincoat, grinning suedes, wicked schoolboy smile—and the feeling that came after?

At least they found Haston's body and somebody, Moriarty, saw him buried. You thought it didn't matter about Haston—he'd none of the innocence of Smith, he'd been away from the High Street too long, he'd spent too much time with the worshippers of money and fame—but then you saw the newsreel of Moriarty carrying the coffin through the snow and then it mattered. The indomitable giant, his great head bowed, shuffling up through the drifts with the front end of the stretcher and the black coffin swaying past the camera made you crack.

Now you wish you'd gone, don't you? You wish you'd mortgaged your meaningless house a bit more and gone. Well, it's too late. Sometime soon you'll be walking in the City and there he'll be—loping along in his big boots, long hands slotted in pockets, shoulders hunched, the big wolf grin and the North Wall eyes, ready for anything. But he won't really, will he?

You remember that time when you both hitched to the Ben, you got there first and he had the key? You kipped in the shithouse, threw the Elsan outside and cursed him. Four o'clock in the morning, a big blue shiny morning, the door burst open and there he was, stripped to the waist cracking that huge grin and waving the key in front of you. Or that other time when you stood all the way from Paris in a train to Chamonix, stumbled out of the station and didn't know a soul? You turned a corner and he was coming towards you like a golden greyhound, sunglassed and sandalled, just back from the Eiger and who could mistake that smile?! Or the time you tried that horrible route of his on the Tannery Bridge, 'grade six sustained' he said, and you quivering on the final miserable fingerhold while he grinned down the parapet and held out a merciful hand? Well these times are all gone now, for you and for him, and won't be again. Except, once in a while you'll get that kick in the guts that tells you it's a dream and you're going to wake up and whenever you go moping about the old wynds and closes there'll be the feeling at corners and the feeling that comes after.

Remember Scott, sitting in some dreary single-end of a studio staring at the camera like a poleaxed bull while the blathering B.B.C. imbecile asked if he ever really knew him? *What does knowing matter,* (you felt like screaming)! He's gone and, with him, a long loping stride, narrow hips, wide shoulders, a lipless grin and bright blue bivouacked eyes.

ROBIN N. CAMPBELL.

PROCEEDINGS OF THE CLUB

Easter Meet 1976—Kinlochewe

THE Easter Meet was based at Kinlochewe with quite a few members and guests at the Ling hut.

The weather was somewhat mixed—very wet on Saturday, much improved on Sunday and excellent on Monday. Parties were out every day and ascents reported en route to and at the meet included the following: Meall na Cuaich, Geal Charn, Sgòr Gaoith, Càrn Ban Mór, Meall Dubhag, Mullach Clach a' Bhlair, Slioch, Fionn Bheinn, Meall a' Ghuibhais and Beinn Eighe.

Present were 22 members and 10 guests: The President, J. M. C. Aitken, J. F. Anton, J. H. Clark, W. L. Coats, R. R. Elton, R. G. Folkhard, J. M. Hartog, J. N. Ledingham, R. C. S. Low, J. R. Marshall, H. H. Mills, M. Morrison, P. D. McNicol, D. H. McPherson, T. Nicholson, G. S. Roger, R. R. Shaw, W. T. Taylor, B. G. S. Ward, J. A. Wood, F. R. Wylie. Guests: J. Broadfoot, W. Donaldson, W. Duncanson, C. Elton, J. Fowler, J. W. Marshall, J. Nicholson, M. Shaw, C. Simpson and L. Watson.

It was a very enjoyable meet and we thank Mr McBrearty and his staff for looking after us so well.

New Year Meet 1977—Glencoe

THE Meet was based at Glencoe Hotel with many staying at Lagangarbh hut.

The weather and winter conditions were superb apart from some deterioration on Monday. It was a most enjoyable and successful meet. Parties were out every day making full use of the wonderful weather and sometimes descending in glorious moonlight.

Ascents reported included the following: Meall a' Bhuridh, Sgùrr na Ciche, Mullach nan Coirean, Na Gruagaichean, Beinn Fhionnlaidh, Garbh Bheinn (Kinlochleven), and Buachaille Etive Mór. Also traverses of Ben Cruachan, Gearr Aonach with Stob Coire nan Lochan, and Beinn Bheithir, and quite a few skied on Meall a' Bhuridh in perfect conditions.

Present were 23 members and 3 guests: The President, D. J. Bennet, B. S. Fraser, C. C. Gorrie, H. Henderson, J. N. Ledingham, H. McInnes, I. D. McNicol, K. Macrae, H. H. Mills, D. M. G. Niven, I. H. Ogilvie, G. S. Peet, G. S. Roger, C. Ross, I. H. M. Smart, D. Stewart, M. Taylor, W. Wallace, C. B. M. Warren, T. Weir, G. A. Whillans, F. R. Wylie. Guests: N. G. Hetherington, R. R. Hollingdale (M.C.S.A.) and A. Jones (A.C.).

It was a truly memorable meet. Our grateful thanks to Mr MacConnacher and his staff for the excellent service and a most comfortable and enjoyable week-end.

At the foot of the Etive Slabs—our new Hon. Treasurer keeps his hand in with a gear check   August 1976

Lagangarbh gets roof repairs   August 1976

Photo: D. J. Bennet

Reception, A.G.M. and Dinner, 1976

YET again we found ourselves in the George Street catacombs. Last year's dash for open country had come to naught—temporarily anyway. There is something ironic in sitting in a stuffy overcrowded Edinburgh cellar looking at slides of Scottish scenery. H. M. Brown's one-man view of Scotland was notable both for the breadth of vision in his commentary and for the high quality of the slides which were shot at psychedelic speed before our eyeballs by Charlie Gorrie—surely the fastest projectionist in the East. A fine show and a timely sermon for the Ultramontanists among us.

Emerging briefly from the anaerobic depths we were revived by the best provision of sandwiches and buns for many a year. Scones like these were thought to be extinct—Edinburgh does have its compensations.

Down again into the depths for the A.G.M. For a while this looked like being a remarkably tame and expeditious affair with the monotony only being relieved by a little gentle chiding of our worthy Secretary for his tendency to edit reports. Jim Donaldson, making his last report as Treasurer after a long and successful run, had to admit to a slight deficit on the accounts but in view of his wizardry over the last fifteen years no one was disposed to criticise. Bearing in mind the rate of inflation during the last few years Jim has worked wonders and passes on to be a Mandarin of the Golden Button with the sincere thanks of the Club. In making his report Jim explained the nature of the mysterious Snart bequest but could not explain, nor can anyone, why the Club had been singled out to administer it. The inevitable sub-committee is considering how it may be honestly used as we appear unable to divert it to the benefit of the Club.

The first rumble of the approaching bureaucratic herd came with the news that the Club would be issuing Membership Cards in order to allow non-ratepayers of Edinburgh to borrow books from the Club library when it is (eventually) installed in the Edinburgh Central Library. During the reports the activities of the National Trust for Scotland in Glencoe and elsewhere drew some adverse comments from the body of the hall and our representative on that body will be asked to make plain the Club's point of view on the conservation of mountain areas. However it must be recorded that the new 'Visitor Centre' in Glencoe received favourable as well as unfavourable comment. On the general question of landscape despoliation the beam in our own eye (in the shape of the Lagangarbh power line) was firmly pointed out by Sandy Cousins. Touché indeed Sandy—not to mention sixty scarlet cylinders somewhere else.

Bill Young was given well-deserved thanks on resigning as Convener of the Huts Sub-committee and George Wilkinson also received honourable mention for his services. (Bill's spell of office saw a notable surge of activity in hut extension and maintenance which the new Convener has no intention of emulating).

The only contentious point of the meeting arose when the Secretary raised the question of supporting the Mountaineering Council of Scotland's new draft constitution and its policy of approaching the Scottish Sports Council for financial grant. We are apparently faced with the prospect of requiring a full-time secretariat to run Scottish mountaineering. Coupled with this was dangled the bait of perhaps expedition grants to the tune of five hundred pounds (gasp!) if we were to gain S.S.C. support pro rata with that given by the Sports Council in England. Despite this lure, and although it was generally agreed that some financial support for the Secretary of the M.C. of S. was more than justified, the prospect of tangling with the bureaucracy to get it was repugnant to a section of the meeting. Despite much debate, during which Bob Grieve confessed to having, after much thought, changed his views to favour an approach to the S.S.C., a group of reactionaries could not be convinced that there wouldn't be a worm in a Government apple. On the matter coming to a vote the gerontocracy prevailed as usual and the reactionaries of the younger generation were heavily defeated.

Of the dinner there is less to be said except to note that the food was of a higher standard than some recent efforts. Alec Small signed off a notable Presidency with a pungent and humorous speech in his best Wee Jake style which nevertheless indicated a concern for the future of the Club.

Iain Smart dissected the Guests and Kindred Clubs with professional skill blended with tact and a whiff of nationalism. Robin Collomb, deputising at short notice for the absent E. A. Wrangham, made a graceful reply. The eighty-eighth dinner came to a close and a well-fed congregation gradually drifted out into the snow.

J.M.C.S. REPORTS

Edinburgh Section.—The Section has been going through a period of losing some members and unfortunately not attracting new recruits which leaves it down in numbers this year. Nevertheless it has been a successful year with well-attended Meets and a large number of worthwhile routes climbed, both in summer and winter. There were no particularly ambitious or inaccessible Meets but our visits to the traditional areas were as individually different as they always are. All in all seventeen official Meets were held. In addition, week-day evening climbing in the summer was as popular and entertaining as usual, especially at Aberdour when the tide happened to be in.

The Dinner was held in the Coshieville Hotel west of Aberfeldy, and was voted as perhaps one of the best dinners for a long time. We had an excellent meal which was enjoyed by all concerned and our thanks go to Mr Reed, the proprietor, who managed to get his chip slicing machine jammed full on!!

Lastly we should like to pay tribute to one of our past members who was very sadly killed in the Alps earlier this year. Dougal Haston was a great loss to every mountaineer. His ability must have inspired many of us to go on to better things.

Hon. President, Mike Fleming; *Hon. Vice-President,* Jim Clark; *Hon. Member,* Ian M. Ogilvie, o.b.e.; *President,* Alistair Borthwick; *Vice-President,* Fraser Fotheringhay; *Treasurer,* Bill Myles; *Hut Custodian (Smiddy),* Jim Clark; *Committee Members,* I. D. Brodie, A. Dunn, J. Fowler, D. More, R. Phillips. *Secretary,* Pete Myles, 59 Morningside Park, Edinburgh, EH10 5EZ.

Lochaber Section.—Membership is down slightly on the record figure for 1975, due to some of the members leaving the area. The number of new members is running at the same level as last year and promises well for the future.

Once again all the outdoor Meets have been very well attended, as have the varied and interesting slide shows over the winter. A large number of local members were active over the winter season, particularly on Ben Nevis, and numerous routes over a wide spectrum of difficulty were ascended.

Steall Hut is still proving a popular and valuable asset to the Club and full use of it was made over the winter season by members of other clubs. There was a record attendance at this year's A.G.M. which is an indication of the interest shown by members in Club affairs and proposals from other bodies affecting mountaineering. The Club is increasingly being drawn into 'mountaineering politics' and is concerned at the increasing interference and encroachment of bureaucracy both from outside and within mountaineering circles on the mountaineer. It is hoped that the Club will continue in the future to keep a watchful eye on all developments and act as a 'backbencher' to all proposals.

Office bearers—Hon. President, J. Ness; *President,* W. Adam; *Vice-President,* D. Watt; *Treasurer,* W. Adam; *Hut Custodian,* E. Kay; *Secretary,* L. Houlker, 30 Camaghael Road, Caol, Fort William.

Perth Section.—Membership has been strengthened by an influx of young active blood, although the figures show a decrease by one on last year's total to 59. During the year thirteen meets were held of which eight were weekend and five were Sunday meets. Most meets were well attended and the average was up on previous years. There has been some increase in rock-climbing during the year, precipitated by a decision to hold a meet in Glen Brittle, the first such by our Section for some time. Hill walking is still, however, the main preoccupation of most of the members of the Section and this aspect continues to thrive.

Our Section's Annual Dinner was again held in the Killin Hotel, and an excellent meal was followed by entertainment in the Fearnan Outdoor Centre. This was the best attended meet of the year and was, as usual, a great success.

The Joint Annual Lecture with the Perthshire Society of Natural Science, was delivered by one W. D. Brooker. His excellent, illustrated lecture on the History of Scottish Mountaineering was well received by a capacity audience.

The A.G.M. was held in Perth in November. After the evening's musical chairs session the Club decided not to renew its membership of the Perth and Kinross District Sports Council as the interests of the two bodies rarely coincided. After a short debate the meeting agreed that an increase of 50p annual subscription was not unreasonable when considered in the light of spiralling costs. The charge made for the *Journal* was also increased in anticipation of a rise in its cost.

The death of one of our Honorary Members, Jimmy Grant, came as a shock to us all. Jimmy had become something of a Grand Old Man among us and we miss him.

Office bearers—Hon. President, Chris Rudie; *Hon. Vice-President,* John Proom; *President,* Joe Stewart; *Treasurer,* Iain Robertson; *Secretary,* John Reed, 9 Burnbank, Bridge of Earn, Perth.

London Section.—The Section again enjoyed a year of mixed activity and success. Because of our widespread membership, costs are becoming prohibitive in many cases for regular trips to the mountains. So much so that full cars to Scotland or even the Alps are probably viewed with more favour than travelling light to Wales or the Lakes. This situation has been further reflected by the popularity of our meets in Scotland and our recent activity in Europe.

Glencoe was the venue for our main winter meet, but the conditions were no better than on our three Welsh winter weekends. The year however developed into one of the driest on record, culminating in a particular week in September when the Welsh crags were all but empty by noon each day, everyone having taken to the beach or llyns.

Our Section cottage, Glanafon, received some attention over the year. The infamous spring bunks have been laid to rest and members and visitors alike can now enjoy comfortable mattresses on a hardboard base. Free lighting and cooking has been installed as have two paymeters for gas fires. Fairly substantial improvements are proposed for the coming year.

Membership of the Section remains around the mid sixties with the usual proportion of late subscriptions.

The Section A.G.M. & Dinner was held at the Waterloo Motel, Betws y Coed and although a very modern hotel, it catered well for climbers. Our evening was livened up by having two pipers on show and a rescue alert thrown in for good measure. We were represented during the year at the Whole Club A.G.M. & Dinner in Fort William, the Glasgow and Edinburgh Section Dinners and the B.M.C. South East meetings.

Office bearers—Hon. President, J. Della Porta; *President and Treasurer,* D. Edmunds, 67 Bourton Road, Olton, Solihull, West Midlands; *Secretary,* H. Jordan, Waytes Cottages, Layham Lane, Keston, Kent; *Hut Bookings,* Staff Sgt. W. Wheeler, M.V.E.E., Sgts. Mess, Rhine Barracks, Aldershot, Hants.

S.M.C. AND J.M.C.S. ABROAD

North America

JIM MESSER is in Newfoundland and has been climbing with Chris Greensmith (formerly St. Andrews U.M.C.). He tells us that his local cliffs are only about 200 ft. but produce excellent winter conditions with plenty of ice and have yielded them a number of excellent hard winter routes. They have been using skidoos for access (*pace* Dutton and Watson). The scope for climbing in Newfoundland seems enormous—more next year.

ROBERT J. WATTERS (J.M.C.S.) writes, 'After being based in that well-known mountaineering centre of Cincinnati, Ohio, for nine months I managed to be transferred by my Company to Alaska, for consulting work on the trans-Alaska oil pipeline. Although initially the assignment was for three months, it fortunately ended as almost two years. Apart from contending with the varied climatic/environmental/working conditions during 1975-76, the following mountaineering trips were made during this time.

'August 1975: to the Selkirk Mountains (British Columbia) with Andrew James (S.M.C.), where five rock/snow dummits were obtained. July: several small peaks climbed in the lower Muldron Glacier/Anderson Pass region of Mt. McKinley Park, Alaska. March 1976: a pleasant week's dog sledging spent in Mt. McKinley Park. April: some ten days spent in a fruitless attempt on Mt. Marcus Baker, 13,134 ft., in the Chugach Mountains, Alaska. After being deposited by ski-plane on the Knik Glacier, severe weather developed on the third day, and dogged the four-man party during the next seven days, requiring much snow cave digging to ensure a measure of comfort. December: Mt. Citlaltepec (18,200 ft.), Mexico, a pleasant peak climbed while driving through Mexico en route to South America.'

Africa

BARCLAY FRASER writes, 'On a visit to Tanzania in October I climbed Mount Meru (14,978 ft.) from the west side. Our party consisted of Kristin Barnett, a V.S.O. in Dar-es-Salaam, an athletic young woman, and her two handicaps, my ageing self and her father, Chris Maclennan, even older and with a leg that refuses to bend. Kristin had previously arranged for a jeep from the nearby town of Arusha and, since guideless parties are not allowed in the Meru nature reserve, had hired two guides from Olmotony Forestry School below the mountain. In any event the guides, available only at weekends, though they were useful in pointing the way through the forest, were a bit of a nuisance above the tree line. We picked them up after lunch on the Saturday and continued by jeep up a rough forestry road through pine plantations, passing on the way the highest point where water can be got.

'Thereafter we tramped up delightful winding tracks through tropical forest, intent to reach the open before darkness brought out the wild animals whose traces were periodically evident. Towards the end the path became a series of steep dust slides, toilsome for those with heavy rucksacks—the guides do not act as porters—and pure Hell for one-legged men. Just before night fall, however, we emerged and pitched our tent at above 10,000 feet.

'At 1 a.m. Kristin and I together with a band of forestry students who had attached themselves to our party, set off leaving Chris to see that the local Masai did not make as clean a sweep of our camp equipment as they had made of the climbing hut that once stood there. Apart from very easy rocks near the summit this whole face of the mountain is buried about a foot deep in very fine, very unstable, black volcanic dust. After struggling with this for some time I began to go weak at the knees and feel sick. The Africans went on—except for two who had fallen out already—and Kristin, carrying our joint rucksack, tramped out footsteps for me and periodically sat beside me till my retchings ceased; after which I went better—till the next time. The views from the summit ridge, however, straight down into the crater and over the sea of cloud to the snows of Kilimanjaro were heart-uplifting and stomach-settling, and the descent on seven-league boots down the yielding surface with a plume of black smoke floating out behind was fast and exhilarating.

'At the camp, which had not been removed by the Masai, we poured the dust out of our boots, but our clothes remained impregnated with the stuff for many a long day. Chris managed the forest descent remarkably well and by early afternoon we reached the jeep which had come up to collect us.

'Kristin tells me that the going on Meru is much worse and more continuously bad than on the screes of Kilimanjaro. There is, however, an alternative route up the north side of Meru from Pyrita Farm which is alleged to be better. That I can well believe.'

HAMISH BROWN spent several months in Morocco in 1976. He writes, 'With Charles Knowles I visited Mischliffen in the Middle Atlas, an area of old volcanos, great cedar forests and parties of apes—not the usual for ski-mountaineering. One all-day trip was done to Jbel Hebri, but it is really a magnificent Scandinavian-like landscape just made for langlauf. Next time! The long drive to Marrakech led on to Oukaimeden, the ski centre, for some pisting and a 15-hour double traverse of Attar-Tamaskaout, easy climbing, but deep snow. Ras and Timesguida n' Ouanoukrim were done, adding Dave Morris—and also later by an Eagle team, both these groups climbing several of the classics. I wandered off across the spine by the Tizi n' Ouagane to descend the Agoundis but was lured to the ridges and peaks beyond, crossing the Tizi n'Zaout to traverse Adrar Tirkout, probably new for British folk. Superb bivies and exit down the Agoundis in spring colourfulness. A larger party were generally messed up by storms but the Eagle Ski Club friends had better luck. Good days at 'Ouki' to acclimatize, then passes to Imlil and up to the Neltner from which several peaks were climbed, including a traverse of Jebel Toubkal, 4,136 m., Morocco's highest, up the Ikhibi Sud and from Tibherine, down the Ikhibi Nord. Akioud was also climbed. All visits to the Neltner ended with ski-ing down to Sidi Chamarouch for it was a year of frequent and heavy storms. A respite in Ourzazate was followed by a happy B.F.M.C. gang of friends; by splitting up a great deal was done. Five of us crossed to Tachddirt and then in one day crossed the Tizi Tachddirt (3,172 m.) and descended the whole Ourika Valley, the wildest imaginable. From there we made probably the first British ascent of Adrar Meltzen (3,595 m.), a fine peak well to the east, defended by lack of map, tortuous gorges and giving two bivies in deep snowfall. It was the first big hill for Anne Bain, Janet Gilholm and Susan Cooper who made up the team. It is planned to return in February-May 1978 with further exploration in the east, a visit to ski in the Rif Atlas, a week's langlauf tour from Mischliffen, a two-week mule/ski crossing of McGoun (see Donald Mill, *S.M.C.J.*, 1973) and also a bird-watching trip. All privately-arranged small parties; anyone interested, do get in touch.'

The Alps

DONALD MILL, with PETER STOKES, IAN CARTER, LEN SMITH (all J.M.C.S.) and Ian van Hinsbergh, were at Zermatt for a fortnight in July. 'In 1975 the burns babbled merrily all night at over 4,000 metres. In 1976, fresh snow at 2,000 metres. Rimpfischhorn and Alphubel were snatched while everyone was fogbound in the valleys and we had all the Mischabel and the Monte Rosa to ourselves, but they were there in their thousands when we traversed the Feekopf and Allalinhorn. Then the Younggrat all the way from the bottom, true Scottish winter conditions at the top, and on the easy way off the naughty avalanche had us. Windslab, at the end of July. Indeed.'

PETE HODGKISS, TED MADEN, Clive Laviolette, and GEORGE WILKINSON were at Zinal and in the Gran Paradiso region from the middle of July until August 5th. 'After two easy training walks at Zinal we fled from the continuing bad weather and the extortionate prices, and crossed the Grand St. Bernard to camp in the Vallon di Cogne, where we enjoyed 14 days of near perfect weather.

'We drove round for the voie normale on the Gran Paradiso to Pont in the Val Savaranche, still undeveloped despite fears voiced in a previous report (*S.M.C.J.*, 1971, *xxix*, 397) anent the road being driven South through the hills to Ceresole and providing day access from Turin: this road shows no sign of being completed in 1976. This was a long, easy plod from the Vittorio Emanuele hut, made notable by perfect visibility around the compass and by the hair-raising antics of the Italians on the narrow, summit ridge. On the same day Ted Maden soloed the Punta Ondezana from Cogne.

'Having made his annual ascent, Clive Laviolette returned to Brussels and George Wilkinson left shortly afterwards. P.H. and T.M. then climbed the Grande Serraz from the Vittorio Sella hut, meeting on the summit a Belgian, with guide, another summit-a-year man whose 1975 top had been Cairngorm; up and down most of the E.N.E. ridge of the Grivola from the Balzola bivouac—the latter proving a devastating 7-hour hut-walk; the Torre del Gr. St. Pietro from the campsite—a most satisfying and varied climb to a fine summit; and lastly a traverse of the Grivola by the North Ridge from the Gr. Nomenon chalets—a superb expedition with the Nomenon ice-fall being much more serious than the West Col guide book (1968) indicates and giving several hard ice-patches: descent was by the voie normale on the S.E. face which lived up to its reputation for stone-fall and must be an evil place when other parties are above.

'The region has much to commend it in that the weather appears to be generally better than the Mont Blanc range and the Valais region and also for the reasonable cost of camping, huts, and food, e.g. camping dues were less than half those in Switzerland; the two main huts provided bed, and a simple evening meal of soup, bread, and wine for £1, and there were several free bivouac huts which seemed to be little used; and Italian food had an average cost equivalent to that in Britain. Another attraction of the region was the surprising lack of people on the mountains—with the exception of the Gran Paradiso, which being the highest mountain completely in Italy, is very popular, we met only two people during 5 climbs most of which, in perfect weather. One drawback is that no wild-camping is allowed in the region (a national park) and the official sites, though having excellent facilities, were very crowded.'

R. N. CAMPBELL, *en route* to Salzburg, broke his journey to make a five-day visit to the Valpelline in late August. This valley is quite accessible and well-suited to quick solo visits, the peaks being low and the glaciers innocuous. From the splendid (free) campsite at the Essert lake just below Dzovennoz (1,600 m.) he climbed the 3,000 m. Aiguille de Crete Seche, a simple rock peak. On the following day he made a rather punishing 10-mile march to the Bivacco Praderio (2,450 m.). This was also excellent (and free) but (*contra* Pennine Alps Guide) contained no stove: neither did Campbell's rucksack. On the next day the Dome de Cian (3,351 m.) was climbed by the normal west flank—a terrific route, full of interest and very exposed on the final summit dome. Puffy clouds drifted past the summit, exposing now the Matterhorn, now the Bouquetins, now the Grand Combin: this latter peak looks particularly impressive from the Valpelline/Valtournanche chain, showing an enormous face of clean red rock to the south-east. On his final day the enforced cold diet and threatening bad weather led him to abandon the south ridge of the Punta di Fontanella (3,384 m.) a few hundred metres below the summit.

BILL YOUNG and DREW SOMMERVILLE planned to have a long weekend together in the Gran Paradiso. 'Base Camp was established in the rain above the Vittorio Emanuele Hut under an excellent boulder which combined magnificent views, when the cloud permitted; running water, when it rained; resident mouse; and true Scottish economy—nae hut fees. The following day dawned hopefully and a reasonably Alpine start was made. Ciarforon by the North-East Ridge was the target with the possibility of doing La Tresenta if Ciarforon didn't provide a long enough day—there's nothing like optimism and ambition to tempt fate. Crossing the glacier presented no problems but route-finding on the rock ridge was tricky—the 'heap of boulders' syndrome being reminiscent of our own 'North-West.' Then came the calotte with worsening weather—cloud and snow with a bit of wind. Front pointing and two axes was the order of the day with minimal security. The top was reached and no view enjoyed. Retreat was effected by reversing the upward route with snow conditions being significantly worse than on the way up—crevasses being discovered where apparently none had existed earlier. Route-finding again had a slowing effect on the rock ridge and snow turned to rain as height was lost. The glacier had by now had the snow washed off it and resembled a rough ice-rink at high angle—at least the thaw water carved interesting burns in the ice. Return to the boulder provided tea, food, more tea and the acceptance that conditions were not going to improve. End of non-long climbing weekend.'

D. J. BENNET, C. R. FORD and C. L. JONES (with several non-members) skied the High Level Route from Argentiere to Saas Fee in ten days at the end of March and beginning of April 1976. Apart from a broken leg (by one of the non-members) and a few minor avalanches, the trip was uneventful, and the only possible criticism of the weather might be that it was sometimes too hot for comfort; afternoon ski-ing was sometimes very slushy. They used the Verbier variant and climbed several peaks en route, including the Petite Fourche, the Rosa Blanche, La Luette, Pigne d'Arolla and the Strahlhorn.

Julian Alps

HAMISH BROWN reports, 'A long trip with Tilman being abandoned due to ill health I grabbed the chance of going to the Julians, an area long-loved through the classic book of Julius Kugy, *Alpine Pilgrimage* (*Murray* 1934). It is about all you will find in English on a peculiarly neglected corner of the Alps as far as the British go. As it is a continuation of the dolomitic limestone landscape this is hard to understand. The scenery is splendid, the Trenta Valley equals any in Europe, and some of the rock faces are huge. It is both unusually wild and unusually tame for some areas have been left in a wilderness state (and wild in the extreme) and others have been wired and pegged and waymarked so that the mobs can enjoy what would normally be climbers' country. This does allow fine high-level walking and with good huts at altitude the valley can be left for a week at a time, a blessing as the valleys are very steep and deep. Triglav is only 2,863 m. but has a face of 4,000 feet. As the highest it is mobbed by tourists in the summer. (Plaques on the rock show a high fall-off rate!). July was quieter than August. In the two weeks the following were climbed: Vogel and Zabiski, Skrbina, Ticarica, Kanjavec, Prisojnic, Mojstrovka, Razor, Planja, Stenar, Kriz, Dolkova Spica, Gamsovec, Triglav, Kredarica, Rjavina, Cmir. Skrlatika in new snow and no gear gave the only check, and it, plus four or five other fine-looking ranges towards Italy, will certainly ensure a return. Botanically it was also one of the finest places I've seen in the Alps.'

Spain

W. D. BROOKER was in northern Spain with his family during July, and climbing with his son Iain. He writes, 'Our first objective was the Aigues Tortes National Park in the Spanish Pyrenees—"the Enchanted Mountains." Passing through Viella and the Val d'Aran, we camped just beyond the Bonaigua Pass. Our first day was spent in visiting the Lago St. Gerber and traversing the Pics de Seros (2,642) above. The sun shone, before us lay a jumble of red granite spires, rising above contorted pine woods, mountain lochans and flower-spangled meadows. The prospect seemed delightful and the area's reputation for reliable summer weather fulfilled. We were soon to be disillusioned. The clouds were beginning to gather as we drove to the road-end at Espot and thence by an extremely rough jeep track to the Lago de St. Mauricio, a kind of Spanish hybrid between Loch Coruisk and Loch Morlich, which provides a brisk trade for the piratical Land Rover taxi-drivers who ferry tourists from Espot. The following day we climbed the Petit Encantat by its East Ridge before cloud and heavy rain ended our plans to traverse its twin, the Gran Encantat. We retreated to Espot and after two further days of bad weather drove southwards and around the entire mountain area to its western side. The rain was even heavier and sorely disappointed we abandoned the Pyrenees for the Asturias in N.W. Spain.

'From an excellent holiday camp site at Llanes we made three brief forays into the Picos de Europa. These peaks made a powerful impression, a forest of jagged limestone towers, many of them with easy tourist routes to their summits but offering abundant choice of more challenging approaches and traverses. The group is divided unevenly into Eastern, Central and Western massifs and all road approaches seem to pass through enormous and impressive limestone river gorges. A sparse network of jeep roads and old mining tracks gives access to the pastoral green uplands from which spring the peaks themselves, in a nightmare confusion of jagged white rocks. We had a good map but were unable to find a guide book other than one dealing with the tourist routes to a few of the most popular peaks. The attractions of the purely exploratory approach are muted here by frequent dense mists which make blind route finding very difficult.

'Our first visit was by the Fuente Dé cable car which took us up to the high plinth from where we made an en famille ascent of the Pico San Carlos (2,390 m.), an easy scramble. The next trip was via Sotres and a very rough jeep track which allowed us to drive in from the North side between the Eastern and Central Picos. We enjoyed a good if rather short rock climb up the West face of the Cortes (2,370 m.) in thick mist and followed it by the traverse to the Prao Cortes. The next day was clear and the South-east face of the Pena Vieja (2,613 m.) gave an excellent climb of about 2,000 ft. up a great slabby couloir which provided both shade and running water. Our third

visit was to the Western Picos and ended up as no more than a pleasant
mountain walk to the Refugio Vega Redonda when thick cloud frustrated
our objective of climbing the Torre Santa de Enol.'

A. L. CRAM writes, 'My wife and I spent several weeks in June and July 1976
among the Picos de Europa in the Asturias and Leon Provinces in Northern
Spain. Perhaps because of the epic battle at Covadonga and rout of the Moor-
ish forces through the mountains in 722 A.D. and eventually from all Spain,
the majority of visitors are Spanish and, once away from the main centres,
some knowledge of the language is necessary to get along, as few encountered
spoke English. Passage to Santander avoids the congested lorry traffic on the
difficult corniche road east to Bilbao and the French frontier. Sporting,
tarred roads wind round the great tumble of peaks, split into three blocks by
gigantic desfiladeros cut by the ice. The east to west extent is some 40 miles
and that north to south about 20 miles. More than 100 peaks exceed 2,000
metres and 23 are above 2,500 metres, the highest, the Torre Cerrado, at
2,648 metres, is just under 8,700 feet. The spired aggressive appearance of
the ridges is reminiscent of the Cuillin, aficionados of which will be able to
guess the weather, the North Atlantic being distant only 20 miles. With an
ill-disposed swiftness, a dense luminous fog integrates with the shining white
limestone, then, should the fanning stock trails lead one astray into the
splintered curtains of rock, sword-dancing can begin in earnest on the razor-
weathered stone, sometimes under the sardonic gaze of one of the taciturn
Pastores. Then only can one begin to imagine the panic flight of the Moors,
accustomed to open country, through the hostility of this place. Dry electric
storms, followed by downpours, add spice to high camping, indeed to high
motoring.

'Camping is not discouraged and good sites on vegetation, with water, are
to be had between 1,000 and 2,000 metres. Lower, hardly any sites are
available and higher, the rubble is discouraging. Transport is needed, if the
toil of raising heavy loads on foot is to be circumvented. A kind of Land
Rover service operates in certain areas, connecting with local bus services
and a teleferico from the Parador Nacional at Fuente Dé, near Espinama
provides a lift of 800 m. to the upper station at 1,885 m., but no camp site is
available near the station, unless downhill. The teleferico was struck by
lightning in course of our tour and ceased temporarily to work. We found
our short-wheel-base Land Rover the complete answer, although the verti-
ginous, thread-like old mining roads were steep and rocky.

'Seven spartan small refuges are tactically well-placed to serve certain
groups of peaks for rock-climbers, but there are not enough places and too
few huts. Nearly everything necessary has to be back-packed up paths to
these huts, nor is any fuel to be gathered above the 1,000 m. level. Pastores,
it is reported, can be hired, at fees of 1,000 pesetas, to guide parties to passes
and even up easier routes, but this is a lot of sterling, even for a long way.
Three small motel type of refuges, we found useful, can be reached by car,
preferably Land Rover. The Refugio de Aliva at 1,670 m. had clean beds and
good food at reasonable charges, reached up steep grades from Espinama
and proved a good centre for the Central Block and starting point for refuges.
It is possible to camp at the Chalet Real above the Refuge and to drive up
to the col above at 1,890 m.; alternatively, to drive down to the headstreams
of the Rio Duje to Las Vegas, to a good camp site, for peaks on either side
and even on to the new road at Sotres. The road down (and up) is, however,
just passable by Land Rover, over rocks. A second Motel, "Entre Lagos,"
above Lago Ercina, accessible by car from Cangas de Onis, is a useful starting
point for two Refugios in the Western Block, namely Ario and Vega Redonda
at 1,560 m. and 1,610 m. respectively and a third at 2,010 m. at Vega Huerta.
The third Motel is the Albergue de Vegebano, above Soto de Sajambre, at
1,325 m., accessible by Land Rover, centrally well-placed with Pastores

guides. "Motel" is an extravagant term for these very small refuges.

'As provisions are nearly impossible to buy within the mountains, it is important to stock up with food, fuel and petrol at one of the main centres of Panes (N.E.), Potes (S.E.), Riano (S.W.) and Cangas de Onis (N.E.). The local baker at Oseja de Sajambre (Centre S.W.) baked very good bread. Good fresh meat, vegetables and bread and butter in any quantity, are available at these townships, not to mention wine and cheap brandy. I found the Hospedajes de Peregrinos, at Covadonga, a good overnight resting place with fair restaurant. Once or twice we recuperated at the four-star Parador Nacional at Fuente Dé, although the daily charge of 2,500 pesetas was a lot to pay for luxury of a sort.

'It is essential to obtain, at the outset, the one first-class map and guide book (in Spanish) for the Picos, all others are of tourist interest only, otherwise valuable time can be lost looking for centres and huts and, again, a compass is of limited value in a local situation of dense fog and convulsed rocks. Few persons may be encountered above 2,000 m. early in the year. Some we found were already lost. The Picos are reluctant to reveal their numerous routes without extensive foot-slogging, some are simple and others repellent, like the 1,800 m. East face of the Naranje de Bulnes, 2,519 m. No moderate way is visible on any face of this towering spire. We attained a number of tops including the Pena Vieja, 2,613 m., Coriscao, 2,234 m. and Pena Castil, 2,444 m. The last involved some 5,000 feet ascent. From the top, a jagged ridge leads sensationally down and up over the arrow heads of the Pico Carnizos, 2,432 m. and the Torre de Oso, 2,511 m. Visible, very close to Riano, on the arid side of the range, is a striking group of rock peaks. Climbing appears to start near base and there is good camping and water beside the mountains. The Parador Nacional at Riano has closed and no refuge is available, although accommodation of various sorts can be had in Riano. A good centre for rock-climbing and peak bagging appears to be the Refugio de Collado (Col) Jermoso, accessible by long walks from Aliva or the cable station above Fuente Dé, at an altitude of 2,064 m. Nearby are Llambrion, 2,642 m., Torre de Casiano de Prada, 2,622 m., Torre Cerredo, 2,648 m., and numerous others. Only 12 places are available, however. The hut is locked and the key has to be obtained before departure—inquire at Government Tourist Office in local centre, for address of guardian.'

A. L. Cram also contributes the following information anent Guidebooks to the Spanish Mountain Areas. Editorial Alpina, Granollers, Barcelona, publish small paper-back general walking/mountaineering gudebooks covering a number of the popular Spanish mountain areas. These are in Spanish and come with accompanying maps at 1:25,000 or 1:40,000 scale. They are useful and describe the more popular walks and mountains but confine themselves to the easier routes.

Copies can usually be obtained at local tourist shops and Information Centres (prices about 90 pesetas in 1976) or from Libreria Gema c/ Milicias Nacionales, 3, Oviedo, Spain.

The Picos de Europa is covered by two books, I Macizos Occidental, II Macizos Central y Oriental.

The Middle East

A. L. Cram contributes the following note about a visit to Mount Sinai: 'Sinai is very rough and gritty with a severe icy wind and plenty of dust, at least in the hamseen season in March. My impression was that Moses was hurrying down to the knoll where the golden calf was reputedly erected, down the long, long scree slope and tripped and broke the Tables and any climber who has hurried down large scree must feel considerable sympathy with him. I assume he took to the scree in haste as the quick way down.

If he had the same conditions as we had, no doubt his temper was already sufficiently tried, what with the wind and the dust in his face and these heavy stone tablets to carry. And of course he would be able to see what was going on down below from the top of the screes which are about 2,000 feet long. If he had come down the ordinary way he could not have seen the goings-on. No doubt the Tables were covered by the rolling scree and are there to this day. This may seem a pity when they are so greatly needed.'

REVIEWS

Climbing in North America.—By Chris Jones. (University of California Press, 360 pp., 200 illustrations. £10·50). This is an important book covering as it does an enormous yet coherent canvas in tracing the historical development of mountaineering in the United States, Canada and Alaska. Understandably the author has not attempted to cover absolutely everything and has not mentioned Mexico, Newfoundland, the Maritimes and other peripheral areas; he has instead traced the history of American climbing in those areas where significant developments took place. The book embodies an immense volume of research and is competently written in what we would all recognise as real as opposed to 'American' English; understandably so since Chris Jones is an expatriate British climber. As such, he is well placed to draw interesting comparisons between climbing history on either side of the Atlantic. One of the significant things that emerges is the way in which climbing developed separately in different areas—the East, Colorado, the Cascades, Canada and California—with little interchange. Not surprisingly perhaps developments were much slower and lagged significantly behind their European counterparts until comparatively recently. In the post-war period American climbing experienced the explosive acceleration and technical development with which we are all familiar. We have learned from American climbing technology. Let us hope we can also learn from some of the other elements in North American history, particularly the relationship between climbers and 'the authorities.' The references to 'ranger controls,' 'climbing permits,' 'safety legislation' and the like, make disturbing reading. We cannot envisage all such things coming to pass here (conceive if you can of the S.M.C. being appointed as official guardians of the Buchaille with the duty of controlling and issuing permits to the Creag Dhu)! But we had better take heed. There is a wealth of anecdote and many other analogies between the American and our own domestic scene. Readers will have no difficulty recognising the familiar Scrubbernut and Peaheid among the Vulgarians of the Shawangunks; some may even experience a whiff of nostalgia. This book renders good service to the climbing world and particularly to North American climbers who one suspects may be lacking in awareness of their own traditions. It should be in everyone's library, if you have a rich American relative, that is—even if you haven't, it is well worth considering.

W.D.B.

Men, Myths and Mountains.—By Ronald Clark. (1977; Weidenfield and Nicolson. 292 pp., numerous illustrations. £9·95).

Ronald Clark's works on the history of mountaineering include *The Alps, An Eccentric in the Alps* (the biography of the American mountaineer, W. A. B. Coolidge) and *The Victorian Mountaineers*. The present book, *Men, Myths and Mountains*, is a comprehensive history of mountaineeering, consisting of three parts. The first part, Days of Long Ago, commences at a precise point, the ascent of Mont Aiguille on Tuesday, June 26th, 1492, regarded by the author as the first true mountaineering ascent. This section proceeds through

arly climbs on Mont Blanc to the Golden Age of Mountaineering. A novel
interesting chapter deals with the origins of mountaineering in North
rica. The second part, Mountaineering Grows Up, spans the whole
ry of World mountaineering from the Silver Age of Alpine climbing (the
d from the Matterhorn disaster to the first World War) up to the ascent
erest in 1953, a vast remit. The final section, After Everest, covers the
t history of the sport and tries to look at all major developments and
s, including those in the East.

Iuch research has gone into the preparation of the book. The text is
lished with quotations and adorned with historical prints and photo-
s. So here, clearly, is a potentially fascinating book. To what extent
t fulfil the promise of its potential?

he first two parts of the book are absorbing, except for one disappointing
chapter. For the most part Mr Clark has succeeded in combining interest with
detail; accounts of major ascents are interwoven with comments on science,
literature, photography, Victorian lady mountaineers and the origins of
British climbing. Beyond the Alps no major range is omitted, from the
Himalaya to the Andes, from Africa to Antartica, from New Zealand to
Japan. I found the chapter on the early history of Himalayan climbing
particularly interesting. The chapter I found disappointing was 'From War
to War.' The last section of the book was also rather disappointing, with only
one good chapter, 'The Awakening East.' Why was this so?

Mr Clark is clearly interested in the why as well as the what of
mountaineering, in trends and motivations as well as in events. But he
comes across best when describing the events themselves, especially those
that belong definitely to the past, rather than to the present or the transition
from present to past. The book begins to lose balance in the chapter, 'From
War to War.' Nationalistic and ethical problems reared their heads during
this period. These issues seem to preoccupy the author more than the crucially
important Alpine climbs which were achieved. The current mountaineering
scene has become exceedingly complex and multifaceted. The Latest and
Greatest climbs, ethics, television spectaculars, outdoor education, conservation, the vanishing wilderness, all these seem to have overwhelmed the
author, leading him to write such despairing passages as: 'The "Powder Puff
Kids" blowing chalk on smooth patches of rock—which makes "very difficult"
slightly less difficult—the rock carvers of graffiti, and the ubiquitous litter
louts cast doubt on the value of democracy and tend to help to bring recruits
to the Iron Guard of reaction.' Phew! By contrast the chapter on the
Awakening East is straight documentation and, like the earlier parts of the
book, is interesting and readable.

A few other points are worth mentioning. The book is primarily about
Mountains, secondarily about Men, and hardly at all about Myths. It is not
a book about one's local climbing grounds or favourite heroes. Climbing in
Britain does not receive detailed or particularly good coverage. Only rarely
do individual mountaineers attain prominence. Interestingly, one who does
is Mallory, who emerges both as the strong man of Everest in the 1920's and
as a sensitive writer on the motivations underlying the sport. One learns that
not only did Mallory say 'Because it is there.' He also wrote, comparing
mountaineering with music, 'There may be inconvenience, and even damage
to be sustained in devoting time to music; but the greatest danger is in not
devoting enough, for music is this man's adventure.'

A related point is, could we not have had references to this and many
other quotations from the literature (such as Lito Tejada Flores' well known
article, 'Games Climbers Play')? The bibliography, though substantial, is
confined to other books, and does not relate directly to the text of this book.
Specific references, especially to journal articles, would have been most useful.

In summary, this is a well produced and entertaining volume, unique in its broad scope and reasonable size. If an important function of an historical book is to awaken in the reader the desire for further knowledge, this book is judged a success by the present reviewer.

TED MADEN.

Memorable Munros.—By Richard Gilbert. (94 pp. £1·25 post free from the author, Stac Polly, Crayke, York).

A Yorkshire lad's account of the ascent of the Munros; and this being a game many play I think the author could have done better than just printing 500 copies. There are interesting tit-bits about Sir Hugh and the Rev. A.E.R. before the writer takes the groups in turn with accounts of his days on them. No tales of mighty deeds on fabulous peaks—and all the better for that! This is something we can associate with; comparing and contrasting, differing and agreeing, but actually knowing similar first-hand experience. For the price it is a good buy, pleasantly laid out and illustrated. The printer's errors hardly matter. Munroists are recommended to obtain this couthy account while they may, before all these stravaiging Sassenachs have scarted down the recent gains given by the O.S.

H.M.B.

Clogwyn du'r Arddu.—By Alec Sharp. (Climbers' Club, 1976).

The third edition of the Climbers' Club guide to Cloggy gives a concise but readable description of this famous cliff. The geology and natural history notes have been omitted, but this is scarcely surprising considering that space has had to be found for over thirty additional climbs. The extreme grade has been split into three tiers and, in general, the climbs have been described in the manner of the most free ascent to date (though one or two of the famous 'cowboy moves' have been retained).

R.J.A.

Journals of Kindred Clubs

Climbers' Club Journal, 1975 and 1976—By Climbers' Club standards the 1975 edition of this Journal is a thin one, in content as well as format; this is acknowledged in the editorial and blamed on the effects of inflation. The articles include a report of the Army Expedition to Nuptse, tales of the Cuillins and the Channel Islands and a not-so-futuristic view of climbing from Peter Harding; but a large section is filled out with transcripts of after-dinner speeches and a momentous debate on women's membership, all surely much better listened to than read. Photographs are few and poorly reproduced. Happily, the 1976 Journal marks a return to the traditional style, a handsome volume with over 100 pages of good reading, impressive photographs and evidence of fine achievements all over the world. Outstanding among the articles is an account by Dave Pearce of two major climbs in the Yosemite Valley; there are also good stories from Kilimanjaro, Everest, Greenland and, of course, Wales. The New Climbs section includes once again the Club's own guidebook areas, which for some years have been dealt with in a separate New Climbs Bulletin. More than 50 ascents are recorded here, varying from Very Severe to Hard Extremely Severe, with one solitary Hard Severe! Other feats in Wales, England and the greater ranges are recalled in a very full Notes section, which ends with a superb commentary on the Buxton Conference. We congratulate the new editors, Ken Wilson and Bill O'Connor, on this first-class Journal and we look forward to others like it.

The Rucksack Club Journal, 1975—Not as good as in past years: there are rather too many articles of a non-mountaineering character, while those that are about climbing are not particularly inspiring, although not without interest. It is intriguing to learn, for instance, that the Australians recognise 10 grades of VS. Perhaps the best of this issue is to be found in the 'Climbs and Excursions' section, where there is an ingenious little piece on roof repair by 'H. Warden.'

Fell and Rock Journal, 1976—Nicely produced, with illustrations of a quality which put our own to shame (although not always correctly labelled). The outstanding articles: a reprint of 60 years back by G. M. Trevelyan on 'Walking' and some pleasant reminiscences by H. M. Kelly. It seems the best authors in both the S.M.C. and F.R.C.C. are those of an earlier vintage!

Irish Mountaineering, 1976—All foreign fare with little to interest a non-member.

Alpine Journal, 1976—The usual mixture of faraway places, science and history with pride of place inevitably going to Everest S.W. Face by Boardman and Richards. 'Mountain Winds' by Connor explains much about mountain weather and Brigham comes down to earth with boot manufacture and its history. Although a profusely illustrated glossy, the reproductions are of variable quality.

New Zealand Alpine Journal, 1976—Well worth reading this. Painfully honest accounts of Jannu N. Face and the problems of expedition organising by its various members. Some pertinent thoughts on the pressures to which mountain regions are subject, even in New Zealand by Massell and Molloy and Avalanches by Dingwall were some of the highlights. Many illustrations complement an excellent Journal.

THE CUILLINS THROUGH FRENCH EYES—Part 2 of *La Montagne*, 1976, contains an entertaining article on *L'Escalade dans les Black Cuillins d'Ecosse.* Inspired by W. H. Murray (' "Ce serait une belle nuit pour faire une course," dit Humble'), our friends visited the *Fissure du Déspespoir,* the *Gendarme Inaccessible,* the *Fissure de l'Aube* and even the *Pilier du Ruisseau Fou.* Not surprisingly, they ran into *brume* and *crachin* and plenty of *petites mouches, insolentes et rapaces* before repairing *au pub* for a *petit lourd.* There they must surely have met old Ronald: 'Nous demandons s'il pleut toujours à Skye. On nous répond: "Eh, non, parfois il neige".'—Bien sûr!

OFFICE BEARERS, 1976-77

Honorary President: ALEXANDER HARRISON, C.B.E.

President: JAMES C. DONALDSON, M.B.E.

Vice-Presidents: W. BENNET and C. C. GORRIE.

Hon. Secretary: D. J. BENNET, 4 Morven Road, Bearsden, Glasgow. **Hon. Treasurer:** W. WALLACE, 22 Bonaly Terrace, Edinburgh. **Hon. Editor:** W. D. BROOKER, 35 Oakhill Road, Aberdeen. **Convener of Publications Sub-Committee:** G. J. TISO, 13 Wellington Place, Leith, Edinburgh. **Editor of District Guidebooks:** A. C. D. SMALL, 13 Hollybush Road, Crieff, Perthshire. **Editor of Rock-Climbing Guidebooks:** A. H. HENDRY, 15 Lauderdale Street, Edinburgh. **Hon. Librarian:** A. C. STEAD, 444 Shields Road, Glasgow. **Hon. Custodian of Slides:** P. HODGKISS, 595 Clarkston Road, Glasgow. **Hon. Meets Secretary:** G. S. ROGER, Glenranald, 1 Pendreich Road, Bridge of Allan, Perthshire. **Convener of Huts Sub-Committee:** R. T. RICHARDSON, 2 Inchlonaig Drive, Balloch, Dunbartonshire. **Custodian of C.I.C. Hut:** G. S. PEET, 6 Roman Way, Dunblane, Perthshire. (Tel. 078 682 3954). **Custodian of Lagangarbh:** J. CRAWFORD, 14 Rannoch Road, Wemyss Bay, Renfrewshire. **Custodian of**

Ling Hut: J. F. ANTON, Sandpipers, 1 Craigdarroch Drive, Contin, by Strathpeffer, Ross-shire. **Committee:** The President, Vice-Presidents, Hon. Secretary, Hon. Treasurer, Hon. Editor, Conveners of Publications and Huts Sub-Committees (all as above) and B. BARCLAY, H. M. BROWN, K. V. CROCKET, B. FRASER, I. FULTON, D. JENKINS, W. H. JONES, W. SKIDMORE and A. C. STEAD.

Journal Information

Distribution: D. F. LANG, 260 Blackness Road, Dundee.

Advertisements: W. H. JONES, 88 Albany Road, Broughty Ferry.

New Routes Editor: K. V. CROCKET, Department of Zoology, University of Glasgow.

Assistant Editor: I. H. M. SMART.

Editor: W. D. BROOKER, 35 Oakhill Road, Aberdeen.

All MSS should be submitted as soon as possible and at any rate before the end of February. Articles and other lengthy contributions should be typed on one side of paper, DOUBLE-SPACED with inch margins. The editor welcomes contributions from members, other Scottish mountaineers and from foreign visitors (provided these last deal with some aspect of Scottish mountains or mountaineering). Photographs are also welcome and should be black and white unglazed glossy prints 6″ by 8″ or larger. All material should be sent to the Editor, address as above.

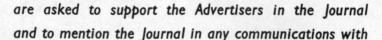